CONCILIUM

THEOLOGY IN THE AGE OF RENEWAL

CONCILIUM

CONCILIUM/VOL. 45

MORAL THEOLOGY

DILEMMAS OF TOMORROW'S WORLD

edited by FRANZ BÖCKLE
THEO BEEMER

VOLUME 45

CONCILIUM
theology in the age of renewal

PAULIST PRESS
NEW YORK, N.Y./PARAMUS, N.J.

PAULIST PRESS
EXECUTIVE OFFICES: 304 W. 58th Street, New York, N.Y. and 404 Sette Drive, Paramus, N.J.
Publisher: John A. Carr, C.S.P.

EDITORIAL OFFICES: 304 W. 58th Street, New York, N.Y.
Executive Editor: Kevin A. Lynch, C.S.P.
Managing Editor: Urban P. Intondi

Printed and bound in the United States of America by Wickersham Printing Co., Lancaster, Pa.

CONTENTS

PART II

BIBLIOGRAPHICAL SURVEY

PART III

DOCUMENTATION CONCILIUM
Office of the Executive Secretary
Nijmegen, Netherlands

PREFACE

Franz Böckle/*Bonn, West Germany*
Theo Beemer/*Nijmegen, Netherlands*

T he fast-moving and far-reaching changes in social and economic structures that we observe in our modern society are bound to affect our basic understanding of our jobs and the responsibility involved in these jobs. The "status" mentality which led to the old class distinctions will have to make room for a more functional understanding. A given social role may well make society expect certain things of the individual, but it does not create any privileges; the value and corresponding claims of a job will be assessed on the basis of the quality of performance and the degree of responsibility. This increasing functional organization leads not only to a lessening of the distinction between dependent and independent jobs, but also necessarily to an overall planning of technological, economic and vocational abilities in the interest of the community. This will inevitably impose limits on the freedom of choice of career, but it will also have the result that the employee will no longer be content to serve as a mere cog in the industrial wheel. Modern enterprises with their complicated and highly valuable technological equipment demand qualified labor. Widespread wealth is therefore no longer the only essential condition for success. Industry and business enterprises no longer achieve success merely on the basis of actual labor involved, and in return for their wider cooperation those employed demand a corresponding share in decision-making.

Apart from these changes in the social and economic structures, there are the hopes and dangers that beset mankind as the possibilities of constantly increasing technological power become clear. Modern man is both fascinated and frightened by the opportunities offered by this technological progress. Many jobs today imply an increased responsibility for which there are no ready-made ethical prescriptions. This makes it all the more necessary for us today to work out some viable basic criteria.

This volume of "Concilium" tries to single out some aspects from this mass of vocational, social and ethical problems. J.-M. Aubert tries to outline the most important changes in modern society in a basic article on their meaning for the attitude to, and function of, a job. Two experts deal with the problems of co-responsibility in industry. By way of illustration we have asked two professionals to make a contribution. The choice, of course, remains problematic, but we have tried to choose professions where responsibility creates special problems. The *physicist* and the *technologist*, above all, must face the question of the possible consequences of their research. The future of the whole of mankind is becoming increasingly dependent on the power of science and technology. Here the otherwise wholly justified basic demand for unhampered freedom in research as the principle by which one works is no longer good enough for professional ethics. Research must be responsible for itself and its consequences. The *physician* is similarly faced with new decisions to be made for new situations. Medical research has given him a previously unthinkable power over life and death. The debate on heart transplantation has shown what a multitude of problems this creates. These problems do not concern only the dispenser and the beneficiary, for they give rise to a whole series of social ethical questions such as the right distribution of the available means for research or the development of medicine. The *judge* and the *civil servant* discuss questions arising from the functional and bureaucratic conditions that have overtaken public life as a whole.

The present unrest among students of various countries shows that the social and professional problems are closely connected with those of education. We could therefore not ignore the problem of the university. This is dealt with in the Documentation section and in an article about the meaning of a Catholic university.

PART I
ARTICLES

Jean-Marie Aubert/*Strasbourg, France*

Profession as a Function in Society

The great transformation signified by the advent of industrial civilization has not only affected nature, modeled and mastered by man, but has profoundly changed the human condition itself in its diverse aspects—biological, psychic, moral, social and religious.[1] In particular, the insertion of man into society by his working activity (not only of a strictly economic order) has been radically modified, and if by *profession* we understand this working activity as engaging the whole human person in a well-defined vital orientation at the service of society, we can then speak of a veritable crisis. Some thinkers are even asking themselves whether the concept of profession is still valid in our day.[2]

Indeed, the separation introduced between capital and labor has, by definition, made labor a near stranger to responsibility in any given undertaking, since labor has become a mere commodity. Likewise, the mobility of employment and the disbanding and migration of manpower necessitated by economic reconversions have often made all professional fixedness aleatory. Finally and especially, the very conditions surrounding technical work (the

[1] On these various changes insofar as they affect the religious life, see C. Brockmoeller, *Civilsation industrielle et religion* (Paris, 1968); *Industriekultur und Religion* (Frankfurt a.M., 1964).

[2] Cf. F. Schneider, *Brauchen wir einen neuen Begriff des Berufes? Viertel jahresschrift f. wissentl. Pädagogik* 32 (1956), pp. 47-60.

piecemeal nature of assignments, monotony, assembly lines, and so forth) have in a way dehumanized it and made it less capable of filling and dilating a genuine human existence. Is there any point, then, in speaking about a person's profession as having a function in today's society? Or is this not a hangover from the thinking of the pre-industrial age? These questions reveal the gravity of the problem raised here. Are the changes which have taken place in society such that they must gradually drain all meaning from the ancient concept of profession? We do not think so, provided this concept is given a meaning in keeping with the exigencies of our times. That is a task which present-day moralists must not shirk if they want to help rethink the notion of profession as a function in society.

Such an investigation should start by examining what might be called the permanent values of a profession. That will constitute the first part of our study. Then we shall discuss the nature and importance of the changes which have occurred in society and which exert a direct impact on the new understanding of profession. The last part will then treat of the difficulties and the specific problems raised when we try to reconcile the conclusions of the first two: how to safeguard the permanent values of profession in the new image which it must assume in a changing society.

I

THE PERMANENT VALUES OF PROFESSION

Human Activity and Self-Realization

One fundamental truth dominates this entire problem; in fact, it forms the basis of any ethic of profession. We are referring to the natural bond between profession and the conditions of existence for the human person.

As an incarnate spirit, the person is first characterized by his capacity to know himself and will himself, to take himself in charge with freedom and full responsibility. But at the same time, he is not made once and for all; rather, he is called to grow toward ever fuller actualizations of the idea of man. To a remarkable degree, he realizes the notion of a living being, in the process of growing: conscious and controlling his growth, he is an historical being.

He pursues this actualization by his free acts; he perfects himself in and through activity which may assume multiple forms, ranging from the immanent action of religious contemplation to the very transitive action of transforming the material world. The ontological nature of the relation between being and doing [3] is revealed in man by the plenitude and the personal realization which he should derive from activity that is worthy of him and of his conditions of existence. And if we consider profession as one of the essential forms of such activity, our chief problem consists in determining how to conceive of profession in terms of the kind of activity dictated by modern civilization. Then we glimpse the generic element of profession: a global activity to which the person consecrates himself and dedicates his existence (*professio*), an activity which he views as a call to him, a vocation (*Beruf*). We shall see later that this is fundamentally the level where our problem is situated.

Human Labor and the Personalizing Function of Profession

Faced with multiple possibilities for historical realization, the person must limit his choice or accept limitation, for the progressiveness of his self-realization requires continuity and, therefore, a certain unicity and specialization in his activity; otherwise, there is scattering and the danger of dispersion and, finally, the failure to achieve personhood. In other words, human freedom has meaning only if exercised within a determinate axis. Freedom cannot be an absolute; it is a dynamism which must work at the bench which happens to be there, with its own exigencies and its own laws. Indeed, man is a being who exists in this world, who is placed in a situation which he must assume.

---

[3] This relationship is expressed in the old axioms *"Agere sequitur esse"* or *"Agens agendo perficitur,"* etc.

Straightway, his nature plunges him into a cosmic and material milieu which penetrates him by means of his body and which he must dominate and exploit in order to ensure his biological exist- ence. This need of transforming the world man fulfills by work—more or less specialized work which presupposes that he is adapted to his specific task (whether or not it coincides with his native aptitudes or personal tastes) and has therefore acquired some facility and competence in the specialty which has now become his own way of existing as a worker. Here we see the specific element of profession as a working activity. The drama of our era, then, lies in the difficulty of reconciling the particularities of industrial work with the fundamental and generic exigencies of the idea of profession, as referred to earlier.

To tell the truth, everything depends on the way the work is carried on and the goal assigned to it. In this connection it is well to remember that human labor can involve various levels of personalization.[4] If we despise or, on the contrary, overesteem the lowest (though fundamental), we run the risk of draining all content from the world *profession*. This is the level of material existence and of the satisfying of economic needs (an average living standard in a given culture). Independently of the moral judgment to be passed on remuneration which is limited to satis- fying these needs (critique of the capitalistic concept of wage earning), work first of all fulfills this minimum vital role of breadwinning, of offering man a means to earn his living. Limited to this function, work remains a "job", a necessary occupation without much bearing on the rest of life. In such cases, obviously, we cannot speak of a real trade or profession; and we must not forget that they are very common in our society, whether it be capitalistic or collectivist, and almost gen- eralized in countries which are in the process of development.

[4] For an overall study of work and its human and religious function, see our *Ethique économique* (Paris, 1969). As for the general moral problem posed by professionalism, it has been thoroughly examined in a beautiful book which we refer to here, once and for all: A. Auer, *Chris- tsein im Beruf. Grundsätzliches und geschichtliches zum christlichen Berufsethos* (Düsseldorf, 1966) (with an abundant bibliography, espe- cially for the German language).

Does this mean that workers in such a situation are doomed never to attain to the permanent values of professionalism? They would be if work were considered strictly in its materiality, as the execution of a purely material task. If viewed in their sheer materiality, a great many specialized tasks in our society are so banal, so monotonous, so picayune and even vulgar that they cannot be more than a means of survival. And yet, as the proverb says so well, "It is no sin for a man to labor in his vocation." That is because the values of a profession are not limited to the tasks it involves, since, in themselves, these tasks can be infused with an ideal, with enthusiasm, as in the artisanship of pre-industrial times, when the craftsman kept in contact with the whole of the finished product and it really came forth from his hands (or as in numerous technical tasks or many liberal professions even today).

At this stage, the Marxist analysis of work can be of some use. Normally, all work is done for a purpose; it is a vital activity, conscious and voluntary—which is why, as we shall see later, finding ways to share responsibility with the workers seems indispensable. Likewise, because of necessary specialization, work is a social deed, a task which makes all workmen solidary and enables them to discover their "generic being". Provided it is accepted by the will and is useful to society, the most banal work—because it cooperates in a global activity and contributes to it in however small a way—can, when thus viewed, open onto personalizing values and onto those which are inherent in social life. We shall see later that this is precisely why the structure of society should make such a perspective possible. There lies the whole problem of the relationship between person and society, which must be rethought in terms of the changes in our world.

Similarly, the Freudian analysis of the relationship between need and desire can prove useful to us. For, as an activity proper to man, work, though it originates in the satisfaction of a need (bringing nature closer to man in order to draw economic goods from it), transcends this purely biological order; or, rather, from out of the need which has been satisfied, work gives rise to the desire for something else, to a dissatisfaction which can drive man along the path to progress and discovery (if he is capable of it) or simply to seeking fulfillment outside of his work—fulfillment which that work nevertheless makes possible, provided it does not exhaust the worker's vital energy. This is the whole important problem of leisure (which we cannot discuss here): leisure considered not as a period of idleness and unproductiveness or even as an after-work activity that has no connection with one's work, but rather as a free activity (not motivated by the need to earn a living), and an activity which, along with the joy and the disponibility it can bring, should allow one to become more aware of the human and social value of work beyond its immediate materiality and thereby restore to it the content of the idea of profession.

The Social Value of Professional Work

That is the essential and delicate aspect of the problem. Only a humanistic conception of society (truly democratic, and not totalitarian) can, as the Church unceasingly reminds us, unify personal and social values in professional work, whatever the transformations undergone by society. Therefore, the delicate relation between person and society needs to be recalled here as a prerequisite for the concrete solutions which must be rediscovered constantly. Society is neither the mere aggregate of the persons who comprise it nor an autonomous entity with an end higher than theirs. Society is already given along with the person, contained in him potentially; for the person is essentially made to open up to others, to communicate and dialogue with them, to enrich himself through knowledge and love. As M. Scheler has said, the fundamental fact of human existence is neither the individual as such nor society as such, but man existing with other men.[5]

Now, this interhuman communication—leading normally to genuine community relationships, with awareness and pursuit of a common goal—begins at the elementary level of all work, which

[5] *Vom Ewigen im Menschen* (Bern, [4]1954), p. 371.

creates solidarity between persons who can provide for their subsistence only if they work together and each of them does his part. We may sigh for the days when it was immediately evident that everyone belonged to a working community (modeled somewhat on the family), so obvious was the participation of each member of the corporation and so close his contact with their common work. Still, we must admit that this advantage was largely offset by the pressure of a hierarchy which enclosed each worker in a rigid status system, and by the absence of participation in non-professional social life (political, for example). Nevertheless, as we shall see later, the difficulties which appeared with the industrial age, though they are of another order, are not such that work cannot play this personalizing role.

We might say that work is one of the hinges that join private life and social life. From one point of view, because of his very labor and the minimum of competence and specialization which it presupposes, the worker is never isolated. He becomes part of a whole—a whole which is very often anonymous and soulless, to be sure, but which affords him security. Now, man, in order to achieve self-realization, needs to feel secure first of all, to know that others acknowledge him and accord him at least a minimum of dignity, which is normally assured by any work well done. Insofar as his development depends on communication with his neighbor, the minimal social integration affected by all work will prove helpful, but it is manifestly not enough if the other levels of his being are not involved or if they are involved but completely cut off from a work life of sheer breadwinning.

From another point of view, all work contributes to the formation of society, which cannot exist unless all do their share and fulfill their respective function, even if unaware or oblivious of it. The enormous injustice of liberal capitalism consists in refusing to see the human character of all work and thereby refusing to have the workers participate both in the common product and especially in the responsibility for the undertaking. Now, to obtain this participation and this acknowledgment of the rights of workers, it is clear that work must be viewed in its total human dignity—that is, in the framework of a true notion of profession. The danger of dehumanization (in capitalistic as well as in collectivist societies) adds to the urgency of truly rehabilitating the professional ideal in a new form.

II

THE CHANGES WROUGHT IN SOCIETY

It has been said that the dawning of the industrial era has proved to be one of the most important historical saltations since the beginning of the neolithic period (with a predominance of rural life, agriculture and the working class, and very slight economic and demographic growth). It would be irrelevant here to describe, even briefly, the principal features of the industrial age and the important changes which it entails for human existence.[6] Accordingly, let us limit ourselves to the main ones which have a bearing on the role of professionalism and the form to be found for it in the new society.

The Emergence of New Structures

The most significant fact is the privileged place which man is gradually conquering, thanks to his ever greater mastery over nature, to whose caprices he was once subject. During the first phase of the industrial era, most men—in the manner of objects—merely put up with this evolution, which frequently made them the slaves of machinery; but now, whether he wishes to or not, man is forced to take charge of this evolution, to rationalize it and assign a goal to it. Doubtlessly, many ambiguities and risks still remain and must not be underestimated. But the place which man occupies in this process today is causing a shift of interests, as it were, in the order of economic and social factors.

Thus, whereas private ownership seemed to be the starting

[6] On this, cf. our *Ethique économique*, Ch. VI, as well as C. Brockmoeller, *op. cit.*, pp. 19-46.

point of the economic and social order a short time ago (whence the importance of the propertied bourgeoisie), work bids fair to play this role in our day. The Church soon recognized the fact,[7] and when Paul VI reminded us that, in this evolution, *having* (the goods possessed) must give way to *being*, he was only pointing out its profound orientation.[8] Indeed, work, as human activity, intimately concerns the being of man, as we saw above. This valorization of work directly affects our problem, since a profession is work insofar as it has been humanized and develops the person. This, therefore, is an invitation to restore to profession its true role in society and, by so doing, find new structures to help work regain all its human dignity.

In the same order of ideas, we see increased importance being attached to human relations in business. In the past, business enterprises were considered solely in terms of the production of new goods, a means of increasing capital, but nowadays regulating human relations between the various members seems to be of primary importance (though outside of any corporative perspective jeopardized by too many totalitarian endeavors). Moreover, even though profit still remains the essential motive of capitalism, the advanced evolution of certain sectors of industrial civilization definitely seems headed in a less materialistic direction.[9]

Lastly, by freeing man from tasks which are debasing or exhausting, modern technology is gradually making his work consist in controlling automated systems. But especially, by increasing production and decreasing manpower, technology—even if the threat of unemployment remains—is ushering in a genuine civilization of leisure, as a form of personalizing activity which can in return animate one's work activity. For leisure thus understood, because it allows a man to stand back from the time he spends working, can help him to integrate that time into his

[7] *Mater et Magistra*, n. 108; *Constitution on the Church in the Modern World*, n. 35.

[8] *Populorum progressio*, n. 19.

[9] This is one of the aspects treated by J. K. Galbraith in *The New Industrial State* (London, 1967).

global existence and so avoid the traumatizing effects of too fragmentary and monotonous a task. Having already noted the importance of leisure, we must acknowledge the full positive contribution of industrial civilization in this area. Eventually, the result should be a greater humanization of society, even if the negative side and the disservices of the technological age seem to predominate in the eyes of certain people for some time yet.

In a word, all these changes are in themselves very favorable to a renewal of the idea of profession and to a better understanding of its social function. No longer is it work, in the sense of a finished and objective product (*perfectio operis*), as much as the technical competence demanded of the worker (*perfectio operantis*) which makes him an artisan who is conscious of social progress. This valorization should also be integrated into a life which is no longer filled with sheer work but which, thanks to leisure, can discover a joy and a motivation that will have repercussions on his work.

A Developing World

Without enlarging on this very timely topic, we should note that one of the most spectacular results of technological and industrial progress has been the possibility of launching mankind on the path of growth in every sphere—demographic, economic, cultural, and so forth—together, however, with the frightful inequalities which affect the immense throngs of the Third World, where growth is negative and the poor become poorer. It is certain that, at the historical level, development illustrates the plasticity of human nature, already expressing itself at the personal level by man's tendency to seek ever fuller self-realization.

With regard to our subject, we must immediately admit that this trait of our civilization creates the greatest difficulty in maintaining the idea of profession. As long as mankind lived an almost static life, where innovation was very rare and where the traditional sociocultural structures changed only slowly (perduring even through political changes), profession established a *status quo,* an almost immutable "state in life".[10] Everyone had his place in a heirarchized social order in which he played a pre-determined role. In addition, as we said earlier, work often afforded a human satisfaction which had an impact on the whole of existence. We can therefore say that in the world of pre-industrial tranquility (with its ominous misery) profession filled its social and personalist role fairly well, even if the lack of political liberty—generally not felt as such—may make us skeptical about the second role. In those days, profession could very well appear to a believer as a highly specialized divine vocation.

But what shall we say about the same problem in a world henceforth dedicated to growing, developing, and always seeking new forms of existence? The demands of growth necessitate a permanent reassessment of structures and modes of work; they entail constant reconverting, dropping sources of production which are only slightly competitive, transferring manpower, scouting for new markets—in a word, a sort of professional nomadism. Lastly and especially, technological progress, with its characteristic acceleration, quickly makes established skills obsolete. In Part III we shall see the conclusion to be drawn from the disquieting fact that the professions have difficulty playing their role in a society dedicated to growth.

A World Which Is Becoming Socialized

In addition to being swept by a vertical movement of growth, our world is also being swept by a sort of horizontal movement of complexification and interiorization, to use Teilhard de Chardin's terminology. This is what we call socialization—a phenomenon which in turn creates further difficulties for the old professional ideal and would almost banish it from the new civilization if we confined ourselves to the traditional definition of profes-

---

[10] It is helpful to point out that the rigidity of the system was not absolute; even if, in itself, the enrichment that permitted one to rise above his "status" was reproved, St. Thomas propounds a more subtle doctrine on this point, as has been shown by W. Friedberger, *Der Reichtumserwerb im Urteil des Hl. Thomas v. Aquin* (Passau, 1967).

sion. Everyone knows that socialization, brought on chiefly by technological progress, is the "progressive multiplication of social relationships" (*Mater et Magistra*, n. 59). A kind of planetization of humanity and of its collective oneness by ever closer networks of interhuman relationships, socialization gives our world a new, more unitary face. It leads us toward unity and the shaping of a common consciousness and culture. It draws men together and makes them solidaristic [11]—with an ambiguity which is no less grave than that of development, for it considerably increases the possibility of clashes and conflicts.

The aspect of socialization which has a direct bearing on our problem is therefore the tendency to reinforce social ties, to make the social predominate over the individual. The delicate relationship between person and society, mentioned above, risks being dangerously warped, to the detriment of the person. Many duties and tasks which formerly were private and could be carried out by individuals are gradually being assumed by the collectivity and often performed better (for example, education, health services and the like). Whence the necessity for society to plan, to foresee what diminishes the margin of free choice, especially in a profession.

To counter this danger, the Church ceaselessly recalls the importance of the principle of subsidiarity, a principle which sets limits to State intervention in the private domain when the common good is not directly threatened. But who can fail to see that socialization leads to an extension of this common good, considering the threat of pressure which can result from the expansion of certain economic powers? (This is the whole problem of nationalization.) Moreover, in an irreversible process like this, it may seem difficult to reconcile the extension of social authority and of its interventions with the free practice of professions which concern all of society more and more directly. This serious problem, which we shall examine later, concerns profes-

[11] For instance, we all feel concerned as to our conscience and our future by the present conflict in Vietnam, whereas France's colonial conquest of the same country in the 19th century left the world indifferent.

sions both as exercised by a person and as organized into an "intermediate body"; in both cases, the difficulty lies in safeguarding the professions' social function (service), their personalizing function and their independence.

III
THE CURRENT PROBLEMS OF PROFESSION

As we said earlier, safeguarding the permanent values of profession amid the changes now taking place in society poses several problems. Limiting ourselves to the chief ones, we would do well to examine them together, since they are related. Because of the general nature of this article, we shall try only to indicate a few broad orientations and shall often raise more questions than we solve, leaving it to the following articles to discuss these matters more concretely.

Profession at the Service of Society

First, let us try to delineate the image which we can form of professions at the present time. This is a preliminary problem in the order of collective representation. One basic characteristic seems to stand out more and more: every profession must henceforth be envisaged from the viewpoint of service. This, of course, does not mean that other, personal ends are not legitimate (profit, for instance), but they should be subordinated to a higher end which, moreover, has always been included in the idea of profession: a function to fulfill in society. As we saw above, because a profession means the doing of some specialized work, the solidarity inherent in that work confers a social character on every profession, even though personal development is to be sought in it.

But in our day, this social aspect must be put squarely in the forefront—again in the name of the personalizing function of profession. Indeed, from one point of view, the social character of present-day work is most evident; socialization has profoundly affected this important human value. The life of many human beings can depend on competence, on conscientious work, on a job well done. Because of the complexity of numerous technological tasks which presuppose a multitude of minute but indispensable interventions, an unknown and isolated worker at his post can have an enormous responsibility toward society. Rail or air traffic depends on a whole complex infrastructure in which, even if automation spreads more and more, the contribution of man (and not always the one who is most seen by the public) remains irreplaceable. The storing and distributing of energy —electricity, carburants, and so forth—takes an army of men. Several years ago, a power failure in one place meant a loss of electricity throughout a large section of the eastern United States. This could have been catastrophic if it had lasted longer and had occurred in the dead of winter. Again, the smallest general strike brusquely reveals how greatly society depends on the world of work.

Thus, even if work has lost part of its human significance (man's efforts directly transforming raw material into some personal creation) or the romantic charm it had in pre-industrial times, and even if it occupies less and less of a man's life, he can and must find personal fulfillment in the consciousness of the social role which he plays, however obscure it may be. The dignity and nobility which he must rediscover no longer reside in the materiality of his task but in the connection between that task and the social life to which it contributes.[12] In this regard we have already said how important today's leisure is in developing such an awareness; for, in his leisure moments, the worker finds that he is only a consumer, the beneficiary of other people's labor, and then he can better understand the social role which he himself plays through his work.

From this there flow several consequences. Awareness of this functional role and the willingness to think in terms of service presupposes a program to reeducate the worker or, at the very

[12] Thus the street sweeper, through work which seems very lowly, contributes directly to the pleasure of living in a clean city.

least, to show him clearly the true dimensions of the work in question, so that its monotony or fragmentariness may become less stultifying, especially if human relations are also fostered.[13] In the capitalistic world, this calls for a complete reversal of policy, when we consider to what extent workers are generally left ignorant, in mind and heart, of the precise aim of an undertaking. But, lastly, it means creating new ways of participating, so as to make the worker co-responsible in a given undertaking and, through it, in the whole of society. (This problem of participation is treated in an article by Wallraff elsewhere in the present volume.)

Another consequence is the ever greater functionalization of the professions. Indeed, since this is a matter of service to society, society has a definite right to examine the structure of the professions. And if a certain profession deals with essential areas of social life (such as transportation, communications, loan and insurance companies, and so on), we can understand that, with the aspect of service predominating, the workers in such a profession should really be at the service of their country by becoming functionaries (not to mention nationalization for the sake of the common good). Furthermore, the complex and onerous technical conditions which many professions require (scientific research, for example, or hospital and medical services) often make it necessary for them to be taken over by the State and for their members to become functionaries.

Lastly, another consequence—related to the preceding one—is the gradual equalization of liberal and non-liberal professions (*liberal* meaning "predominantly intellectual"). Indeed, as a result of technological development, many occupations which were once classified as manual labor are now becoming increasingly regulative and supervisory and, because of the knowledge they require, more intellectual. To use J. K. Galbraith's terminology, many blue-collar workers (laborers) are on

[13] From many quarters we read about the happy results obtained by making the personnel aware of the meaning and purpose of the various tasks performed in each shop.

their way to becoming white-collar workers (office and laboratory personnel). By drawing together workers who belong to different worlds, this equalization preserves them from the individualism of the past and, with time, will facilitate their integration into society.

Planning the Professions for the Common Good

We have already seen that, as a result of growing socialization and the extraordinary complexity of modern economic activity, this activity can no longer, *a priori* and absolutely, be left entirely up to voluntary effort. During the numerous crises which have punctuated its growth (and which point to a host of human miseries), the economy has revealed its inability to regulate that growth. Accordingly, it has often called upon the State, which has gradually taken cognizance of the role it must play due to the magnitude of the process and its close connection with the common good. And the State then exercises this role by means of planning which, in a personalist perspective, should not result in depriving private persons of their rights and legitimate initiative but safeguard the principle of subsidiarity. Designed to promote economic expansion, this planning sets goals to be attained and maps out steps to stimulate companies, to orient and coordinate their decisions. Any democratic plan, then, presupposes a political choice, options for the future (whence the importance of short- and long-term projections), and also the training and educating of economic leaders who, too often, are still imbued with liberalism.

The impact of planning on the free choice of a profession (which used to be the general rule) is therefore evident. Since no modern economy can subsist unless it grows, there exists a wide margin of uncertainty as to the direction and extent of its growth. But, above all, no nation, being incorporated into vaster economic blocs (like the Common Market), can claim to produce everything itself; it is obliged to privilege certain sectors of the economy for which it has more and more natural resources or available manpower, for instance. And, as it looks into the future and considers the common good, each country foresees a diminution or, on the contrary, an increase of manpower in this or that profession. Consequently, it is induced to limit the freedom of individuals in choosing a profession, or to allow and facilitate their migrating to countries where there is greater need for their particular skills. (Here we encounter the problem of the migration of workers, which concerns both the "giving" country and the "receiving" country and, ultimately, the international community.) These necessary restrictions obviously have repercussions on technological and university training, which should normally prepare people for the various professions. Whence the question: Is it right to select candidates for a certain discipline when there is only a small demand for it? (On this and related topics, see the following article by Luyten.) Finally, it should be noted that this planning with regard to choice of profession is more urgent in countries which are in the process of development, where everything has to be created from scratch.

Another consequence of socialization is the necessity for the State to orient the professions, as groups of occupations, toward greater integration into the economic and social whole. This problem is delicate, for many professions, still fearing an authoritarian regime and accustomed to self-defensive reflexes, tend to withdraw into themselves (especially when they enjoy some traditional privilege) and have trouble accepting the idea of either disappearing or being adapted to revolutionary new techniques. Here again we see the importance of education in economic and civic matters.

Can We Still Speak of a Professional Vocation?

We should like to end this discussion by considering a more general problem. In the rigidly hierarchized society of former times, profession clearly denoted a human existence dedicated to some specialized task, usually for life. To this, Christian teaching had spontaneously applied the doctrine of a "divine vocation" proper to each "state" in life. But, as we have repeated throughout this article, modern society, with its constant changing and development, cannot *a priori* guarantee that the professional forms of the past will remain those of the future. The mobility of the professions has become an everyday fact—one which often makes many professional orientations aleatory. If a machinist or an electrician has received sound technical training, he can be taught to work in a chemical company as well as in a textile mill. (This should lead our schools to insist on good basic instruction which allows of diverse orientations.)

As a result, we can no longer say that there exists for each man an immediate divine vocation which predisposes him to this or that profession. A more theological view of the religious basis of work should lead us to broaden considerably the idea of vocation applied to temporal tasks. Man's only true vocation consists in ever more fully developing his personality, his being as a "son of God", in the service of his brothers—that is to say, of society; and although such and such a profession is the particular means of implementing this fundamental vocation (with personal dispositions, historical circumstances and the service of society playing the role of secondary causes), it must be permanently open to the possibility of other tasks. In this way, the idea of profession can still prove useful in helping to solve the eternal problem of the relationship between person and society and, together with that, the religious meaning of temporal involvement.

Norbert Luyten, O.P./*Fribourg, Switzerland*

The Catholic University at the Service of Tomorrow's Society

The choice of this subject in a volume of *Concilium,* which seeks to define the responsibility of Catholics in building the world of tomorrow through their professional involvement, may seem paradoxical for more than one reason.

The University and Vocational Training

First, is it not already a misapprehension to view the university in terms of professional training for future employment? Universities, after all, are not vocational schools and do not wish to be. Whereas vocational schools spring from a pragmatic intention and organize their teaching and research accordingly, universities have always zealously upheld their own strictly scientific character. They obey the imperatives of science, not considerations of a practical order. If they fiercely defend their right to autonomy, they do so because they are conscious of being in the service of truth instead of any pragmatic interests whatsoever. If they desire to serve society, they do so not by subordinating themselves to it and its imperatives, but rather by revealing to it the imperatives which truth imposes. Recent examples have shown us what it can cost universities to be put in the service of a society which has little care for truth. But let us not labor the point. Though, in one sense, the objection is relatively easy to answer, it nevertheless contains an element of truth which must not be overlooked if we would correctly pose the problem of the university in our contemporary society and especially in tomorrow's. We shall have to return and explore this subject in greater depth.

The Catholic University: An Anachronism?

But before going any further, we should mention another objection which is even more likely to occur to our readers when they see the title of this article. We must squarely face the fact that among many Catholics today Catholic universities do not have a good press. If universities in general are being bitterly denounced as institutions that cling to the past rather than take inspiration from the future, Catholic universities are widely considered—even, and I would almost say especially, in Catholic circles—an anachronism, relics of bygone days, still preserved here and there in our present society but doomed to have no place in the world of tomorrow. As a matter of fact, we are told, to anyone who can read the signs of the times it is clear that we are moving toward an increasingly desacralized, profane civilization. No longer able to remain in its ghetto, Christianity must boldly mix in with the world. But that will be possible only through a very far-reaching "secularization" which wholeheartedly endorses the autonomy proper to each area of human activity. Now universities, as institutions dedicated to research and scientific teaching, have nothing sacred about them. By their nature, they are profane institutions. When we want them to be Catholic, are we not going against the current, perpetuating ambiguities, and introducing religious and denominational categories where only the imperatives of science should matter? Are we not running counter to that internal autonomy which the Council affirmed for the diverse areas of human activity? [1] Now if the Catholic university is already obsolete and anachronistic,

---

[1] *Constitution on the Church in the Modern World*, n. 36.

how can we imagine that it might effectively collaborate in preparing the world of tomorrow? Is this not an illusion which should be utterly shattered?

Provided he is at all familiar with the present thinking of a great many Catholics, the reader will not accuse me of having exaggerated this objection for the sake of the cause. We here encounter a difficulty—at least a psychological one—which could weigh on our whole discussion like a heavy burden. Lest we embark upon a dialogue between deaf men, we should take a clear stand on these points right from the start and begin by stating as precisely as possible how we envision the Catholic university today.

The Catholic University and Secularization

Elsewhere we have taken a clear-cut position in this debate which is currently dividing thinkers.[2] While referring the reader to those publications, we shall briefly summarize the essence of our thinking on the question. First of all, we heartily subscribe to the directives of the Council enjoining us to respect the autonomy of the profane sectors of human activity. Unequivocally, it is out of the question to place scientific research under tutelage—even the Church's. In that sense, we therefore say a firm "yes" to what has rather unfortunately and ambiguously been called secularization. The fact is that we must dispel the ambiguity which clings to this term. If it simply means that each profane sector must enjoy perfect autonomy, in conformity with its own nature, we fully agree and readily subscribe to the expression. But if it means that the sacred and the supernatural—or, more concretely, the message of Christ—must be absent from all institutions which are not directly Church-related, then we say just as firm and convinced a "no" to what we can only consider to be an intolerable and intolerant claim. Let us view the matter more closely in regard to Catholic universities.

[2] N. Luyten, *Pourquoi une université catholique?* (Fribourg, 1965), esp. pp. 14-31.

The Right and Duty of Catholic Doctrine
To Be Present on Campus

Many contemporary minds deem it incongruous to mix Catholicism and universities. To them, the result is a hybrid blending of two alien elements, and they can interpret it only as an unwarranted intrusion of the sacred into the realm of the profane, a typical expression of a kind of theological imperialism which has done considerable harm to science.

Let us begin by admitting frankly that there has been theological imperialism and that it has hindered the progress of science. We have only to recall the case of Galileo. Heaven knows how the Church has been criticized on that score! [3] Yet it takes fairly limited wisdom to judge an institution solely on the mistakes it may have made. We should remember that abuse is no argument against proper use: "Abusus non tollit usum."

Against this rather summary condemnation which some of our contemporaries feel they can hurl at Catholic universities, we vigorously maintain that these universities are and will continue to be not only relevant but necessary institutions in our world of today and tomorrow. Far from being hybrid entities doomed to vanish from modern society, they are instead postulated by the very nature of the university as well as by that of the Catholic faith.

No doubt, such an assertion will cause a few readers to jump. We insist, however, that it is absolutely true. In fact, a university, by its very nature, is an institution in which, through teaching and research, human knowledge in all its forms is cultivated. Now, the Catholic Church likewise possesses a body of knowledge; it was entrusted to her by her founder, who commissioned her to teach this truth, to deliver this message to all nations.[4]

We can easily see, therefore, how a bond of connaturality links the Catholic message with the university. Precisely in ful-

[3] Notice has no doubt been taken of the semi-official rehabilitation of Galileo by Cardinal König in the opening address which he delivered at the Congress of Nobel Prize Physicists at Lindau in August of 1968.

[4] Mt. 28, 19-20.

filling their specific function will universities be able to welcome Christ's message as an integral and—as we shall see—integrating part of human knowledge. A Catholic university, then, is neither a contradiction in terms (to quote George Bernard Shaw, who, in the spirit of the times, saw the Catholic Church only as a fundamentally anti-scientific institution, because it is bound up with "dogmatic" truth) nor an anachronism (as in J. Leclercq's rather simplistic view [5]), but an institution which is justified in its very conception. This means at the same time that, in itself, it does not draw its justification from any historical constellation and is therefore not essentially linked to this or that period of history. Consequently, to wish to exclude Catholic universities from the world of today or tomorrow by calling them outdated, is to make short shrift of what is most vital to the question.

A Few Necessary Precisions

But let this be rightly understood. We are not such "essentialists" as to hold that an institution which is valid in its "essence" will necessarily be so in any and all circumstances. Something can be good in itself but unsuitable in a particular situation. Building a school to instruct the young is excellent, yet we should not do so if we lack the material means to carry the project through. Thus, a Catholic university, however fine in theory, may not necessarily be desirable because of political, historical, economic or other circumstances. That such circumstances can be multiplied in our modern world, we readily agree. Still, we maintain that if all Catholic universities disappeared from the face of the earth, academia would lose one of its most essential dimensions, and the Church would seriously fail in her duty, no longer assuring the presence of her message where it should most especially be heard.

Despite what we have just said, which plainly rules out all claims to a monopoly on the part of Catholic universities, some of our readers will remain unconvinced that a Catholic university can ever be justified. They cannot shake off the impression that, when all is said and done, they are dealing with a hybrid institu-

[5] See the work referred to in footnote 2.

tion in which two incommensurable elements are combined: human knowledge on the one hand, and divine faith on the other. We would like to answer this objection briefly, in order to remove, as much as possible, any misunderstanding which could subsist between our readers and us. In one sense, the truth of faith, which introduces us into God's transcendence, is quite incommensurable with the truths which our human scientific research manages to discover. Of themselves, the mysteries of the one and triune God, the Savior and redeemer, escape all human investigation. But these mysteries are entrusted to us. God's message, which makes him known, is at the same time a message to us concerning our salvation and our destiny. It is a truth which should guide us, which discloses to us the meaning of our life, of mankind's vast adventure, and of the entire cosmos. In this sense, this truth, though divine in origin and essence, is an eminently human truth. To deny it its place in the university as a matter of policy, is to fail to recognize the nature of the university, which by vocation must be open to the whole of human knowledge. It would be more than paradoxical if, in the name of human knowledge, anyone were to exclude a message which claims to bring the most decisive and most fundamental truth human knowledge can apprehend.

The Catholic University's Distinctive Service to Human Society

If what we have just said is correct, the immediate consequence is extremely important with regard to the role which Catholic universities must play in human society. Though a university is a place where human knowledge is deepened and taught in all its fullness—insofar as possible, obviously, considering the limitations inherent in all human institutions—the mere juxtaposing of different disciplines will not enable it to answer the vocation to universality which its very name implies. We have too easily forgotten this because of the trend toward ever narrower specialization prevailing in our universities of late. In spite of legitimate and necessary differences in methodology, which give each discipline its proper character, human knowledge constitutes an organic whole. There is a path that leads from any partial truth to any other. One of the university's duties, since this is likewise a matter of genuine knowledge, is to study the multiple connections which bind the various branches of learning to one another. To put it still more clearly, one of the university's most essential tasks is to integrate knowledge not so much as a discipline alongside the others, but as an intention which is more or less explicitly present in all scientific research. Putting slices of knowledge at the disposal of individuals and of society while leaving them the job of integrating these fragments into a valid synthesis, would be a deplorable abdication on the part of the university. The fact that the great majority of our universities fail in this duty should not make us shut our eyes to this exigency which is intrinsic to the very idea of a university.[6]

To the extent that one admits this postulate—and we believe that no one can do otherwise—it becomes evident that only a Catholic university, by consciously integrating the divine message into its synthesis of knowledge, can present a truly comprehensive view of man and the world. Depending on the quality of its professors, the means at its disposal, its resources and so forth, it can be inferior to other universities in its teaching or research in such or such a field, but, as a rule, it will have the advantage over "neutral" universities of integrating the different branches of knowledge upon the vaster and more fully human horizon opened up before our minds by revelation.

The Catholic University and the Integration of Knowledge

For—and this point must be emphasized—a Catholic university is not one where we add to the chairs which exist in other universities a few chairs of Catholic theology. A "neutral" university can do that just as well, and it is precisely what several great German universities have done, for example. To be sure, the presence of a school of theology in a university clearly indicates that theological teaching and research are there considered

---

[6] *Studi Sassareni* will soon publish a study of mine entitled "L'Université et l'intégration du savoir."

an integral part of the university's task. Still, the integrating force and role of theology will be unable to make themselves felt as effectively as they should, since the other departments have no official commitment to the message of Christ. This is different—or, perhaps more correctly, ought to be different—in a university which is Catholic in the full sense of the word. In this context, let us state that we are not here reporting what the various Catholic universities are actually achieving. We are simply trying to say what one has a right to expect from them in view of their specific character. Doubtlessly, the reality often falls short of the ideal. That, however, is not peculiar to Catholic universities; all our human institutions, even the most perfect, are subject to the same failing.

Having said this, we assert that Catholic universities in themselves possess an integrating force which they alone can put into operation. They do so, first of all, as already stated, by the presence of Christ's message at the level of university thinking. By virtue of this fact alone, they possess one more asset than universities which do not have a school of theology. But there is more. When rightly understood, theology has, by its nature, an integrating force which distinguishes it from most disciplines. True, from the viewpoint of source it is a wisdom which comes not from man, but from God. Certain rather hasty minds conclude that for this reason among others theology lies outside the sphere of human knowledge and, by that very fact, is condemned to keep to itself instead of being a factor of integration.

We have already encountered this objection above, in practically the same form. Although revealed truth comes from God, it is an answer to the most fundamental questions which live—existentially—in the heart of man. What is the meaning of this world whose structures we are studying? What is the meaning of human life? What are we doing? Where does man come from, and where is he going? Whereas specialized and scientific research can help to make us forget these basic questions, theology makes us attentive to them and, by its implantation in the Catholic university, renders them present to the other disciplines.

Not that theology would encroach upon their respective autonomy, but each discipline, while preserving its autonomy, forms
part of a greater whole. If, in one sense, the expansion of knowledge leads to further compartmentalization of various disciplines, it also shows us increasingly evident relationships and con-
vergences between areas of knowledge which, at first sight,
seemed utterly foreign to one another. Now the presence of a
living theology, recognized by the other departments as a valid
science in the highest degree (since the professors will normally
share the revealed truth from which theological reflection draws
its inspiration), is of a nature to make these professors conscious
of the intercalation of their discipline on a total human horizon.[7]

Naturally, this ideal can be realized only if a dialogue is instituted between representatives of the various departments and
theology. From observing the concrete situation in our Catholic
universities, we might get the impression that such fruitful dialogue is far from taking place. And we would not be completely
wrong, but neither would we be completely right. Dialogue is not
established only when people explicitly and formally decide to
speak to one another. Through seemingly anodyne contacts,
everyday elbow-rubbing and sheer coexistence on the same
campus, mutual enrichment can and, in fact, does result.
Obviously, however, we cannot settle for that. It is to be hoped
that everyone engaged in constructing a Catholic university—a
day in, day out task—is aware of the part he must play in working out a Catholic *Weltanschauung* which is solidly grounded
and capable of assimilating the contributions made by the different disciplines. May we add that the presence of theology in
Catholic universities normally entails a more thorough teaching
of philosophy, since philosophy is intrinsically necessary to the
development of a genuine scientific theology. Now, philosophy
likewise—and in a still more immediate sense than theology—is
a knowledge that possesses high integrating power. Posing the
most fundamental questions concerning cognition and the reality

[7] See E. Schillebeeckx, *L'Université catholique comme problème et
promesse*, p. 44ff.

which we claim to reach thereby, philosophy explores the common bases of all human knowledge and, by that very fact, reveals the underlying unity of this knowledge.

The Catholic University and the World of Tomorrow

We have dwelt at some length on the subject of integration because, on the one hand, it strikes us as the university's most characteristic contribution to the society of tomorrow, and because, on the other hand, we believe it to be what that society will most need. The fact is that we are manifestly living in a period of transition. A world which once derived its equilibrium from certain concepts, from certain values and forms, is dying before our eyes. An imposing number of factors have combined to change the traditional structures of our civilization radically. Without wishing to attempt a complete diagnosis here—an endeavor which would exceed the scope of this article—let us mention the impact of scientific thought on the modern mind, the growing role of technology in our life, the ferment of ideas made possible by modern communications media, the wide popularity of Marxist ideology, the awakening of young nations, the worldwide demographic explosion, the formation of super powers equipped with atomic weapons, the increasing democratization of our modern societies, and so forth. All this places us before new problems, forcing us to abandon outdated solutions and rethink the questions in terms of wholly new facts. I am inclined to think that we are now drawing the final inferences—and, this time, radically—from the upheavals which have followed upon one another since the beginning of the modern era: the Renaissance, the Reformation, the French Revolution, decolonization, world wars and the like. The young, in particular, feel that until now we have lived by expedients, that we have put new wine into old skins—in a word, that we have too often been satisfied with patching up old formulas, rephrasing them slightly but not really adapting them to totally new situations.

The challenges issued by the young almost everywhere, their rejection of existing institutions, and their rebellion against the

establishment—all of these are so many signs of a profound dissatisfaction with society as it now stands. The extreme forms of
this tendency, which resort to violence and destruction, are inor-
dinate expressions of the same determination to break away from
the rut of outworn forms, of conventions which have lost their
meaning of anachronistic institutions. While deploring the frequently stupid excesses which are associated with this movement
of "renewal" and which often turn it into a demolition project,
we must see these excrescenses as a manifestation of the sometimes groping and fumbling desire to build a new, more just and
more human society.

Now the university is simultaneously one of the most vulnera-
ble institutions and one of the most powerful factors in this
movement, which can be described as a wave of challenge or of
renewal, according to the viewpoint taken. The violence with
which academic structures are being called into question in many
countries shows sufficiently to what extent the university, in its
traditional form, has become a disputed institution. The many
charges—sclerosis, failure to seek adaptation, inertia and the
like—are not always justified, and especially not to the same
degree, depending on each institution. Still, there is no doubt
that a fresh look at the value of existing university structures and
an attempt to reorganize and adapt better to actual needs are of
the utmost utility to our universities.

On the other hand, it is quite evidently the university—
especially through its students—which leads the vanguard in the
battle for a new world. Because they are not yet rigidly incorporated into an increasingly production-minded society and are less
rooted in tradition and convention and more open to the future
and the world of tomorrow, students feel freer to question and
challenge, to make accusations and demands. Of course, there is
in all this a mixture of inexperience, failure to understand, injustice and lack of moderation. Let us hope that these are only the
excesses of an aspiration which is fundamentally just.

We believe that Catholic universities have an important role to
play in this development which questions hitherto uncontested

institutions and ways of thinking and looks ahead to a radically renovated society. In the pages that remain, we should like to suggest the principal ways in which our Catholic universities could make their influence felt.

A More Human World

If there is a diagnosis which can be made without fear of contradiction, it is this: our world, torn by profound and contrary tensions, has lost its interior equilibrium and is painfully seeking a new equilibrium. Granted that the world has never experienced perfect equilibrium since original sin, still there have been long periods when a certain stable order reigned—somewhat in the sense in which M. Buber speaks of periods of *Behaustheit*. Using the same terminology, no one will deny that now, instead, we are in a period of *Unbehaustheit*. Balance and proportion have fled; technology is progressing so fast that a normal person can hardly keep up with it; it provides him with ease and comfort which may very likely smother his higher aspirations; he is thrust into a system of production which threatens to rob him of his personal initiative. And the list could be made longer. Let us not be misinterpreted, however: we do not advocate calling a halt to technology or industrialization or social progress. That would be foolish. The problem is not stopping, but regulating—introducing a human equilibrium into these different factors. But this presupposes a scale of values in which man remains the center of reference. In all the conquests of science and technology, what matters in the final analysis is man. Despite all their excesses, despite the violence and the disfigurations, this is what, at bottom, all the protest movements are clamoring to have recognized. Now, paradoxical though that may seem, the Catholic university is, by its nature, sensitized to this human dimension, which it discovers everywhere. For faith in God, adherence to a revealed truth, does not mean alienation from man, as Feuerbach and the Marxists maintain; on the contrary, it is through God that we rediscover man. The Gospel message is eminently human because it restores man to his dignity as a son of God. Vatican Council II, in its *Constitution on the Church in the Modern World,* tried to show to what extent the Catholic Church views herself as the ideal framework for human progress.[8] In a world torn between divergent interests, we do not need the kind of specialists who are imprisoned within their specialization. We need specialists—men competent in their respective fields—provided that they have a broad horizon and are open to all human problems, far beyond the narrow limits of their specialization. True, no one today can be a universal genius, competent in all domains. But competence is one thing, and openness is another. To construct a more human world, we need men with an appreciation of human values. I believe I can affirm from personal experience that the Catholic university, because it is rooted in a Christian *Weltanschauung,* is a choice climate to make this appreciation blossom forth. Once again, let there be no misunderstanding. We are not claiming that Catholic universities have a monopoly on humanism; in fact, we readily recognize the value of other forms of humanism, even outside of any Christian inspiration. On the other hand, we firmly believe that our humanism, opening onto the transcendent God who revealed himself through Christ, is a more complete humanism and, for that reason, more valid. Universities which make it the basis of their teaching and research are, by that very fact, better equipped to form truly human men.

Catholic universities have at times been accused of serving as a ghetto designed to protect young Christians from the noxious influences of the world. There is some exaggeration in the charge but, no doubt, some truth as well. We do not choose to enter into this question now.[9] Instead, what I want to point out is that Catholic universities, without attempting in any way to be policemen or watchmen, offer their students, along with scientific training, a moral ideal. Here, of course, one must be extremely prudent and make all the necessary distinctions. But I see no harm in neglecting to effect a total separation between the formation of intelligent, competent men and the formation of men, period.

[8] *Constitution on the Church in the Modern World,* Preface.
[9] I have done this in the work quoted in footnote 2.

Once more, Catholic universities do not lay claim to a monopoly in this area either. All I wish to underline is that because of their Catholic inspiration, they do not conceive of the quest for truth apart from human righteousness.

A More Personal World

These reflections lead us to point out another aspect of the service which Catholic universities are called to perform for the society of tomorrow. None of us can say exactly what that world will be like. Some describe it to us in terms of growing depersonalization. As for me, I am convinced of the opposite. True, the weight of the masses will continue to make itself felt—perhaps even more intensely. But unless all the signs are deceptive, tomorrow's society will require from each of us ever greater presence and personal collaboration. Is not the categorical rejection of everything conventional basically a rejection of the impersonal? Is not the profound movement of *aggiornamento,* which is shaking the Catholic Church at this moment, essentially the transition from a conventional religion to a more personal one? [10] Obviously, distinctions are needed here also, but, in the main, this is definitely what it is all about.

What we thus observe within the Church is not an isolated phenomenon. Throughout the whole of human society, we are witnessing a crisis of authority which is only an incised manifestation of the will to be one's own master in an entirely personal fashion. Moreover, in a technicalized and differentiated world like that of today and, *a fortiori,* of tomorrow, there will be need of competent men who can assume their responsibilities. Now it is only a person, in the full sense of the word, who can be really responsible. In this sense also, the aspiration of students to have greater responsibility in university matters is, in itself, a heartwarming phenomenon. This obviously does not mean that all such demands, however extreme and absurd, are to be hailed as a form of student emancipation. Authentic personality does not

[10] See J. H. Walgrave, *Geloof en Theologie in de Crisis* (Kasterlee, 1967), pp. 345ff.

assert itself by refusing to become part of some order. Quite the contrary. Anyone who is truly and fully personal is conscious of his responsibility toward society. Indeed, only in an ordered society can man reach the full development of his personality. Again, without wishing in any way to claim a monopoly, the Catholic university draws its inspiration from an ideal which advocates absolute respect for the human person.

It would not be difficult to cite cases in which Catholic doctrine has stood alone to defend the inalienable rights of the person. But since we are limiting ourselves here to a statement of principle, we should not enter into considerations of fact.

A Pluralistic World

Let us turn, rather, to another aspect of the world of tomorrow, to which the Catholic university, at first sight, seems less well adapted. I am referring to the fact that our society is pluralistic and will most probably be even more so in the future. Is not the Catholic university, because of its one-way denominational ties, in flagrant contradiction with this pluralism, which is so characteristic of our society?

In one sense, there is some truth to this objection, and the Catholic university alone is surely not the answer to the imperatives resulting from pluralism. In our pluralistic world, it is normal and even necessary for Catholics to have a hand, both as students and as professors, in the academic labors of the different institutions in their country. Whether these be private or state universities, neutral or interdenominational, Catholics owe it to themselves to be present and active there. But over and above that, our pluralistic world, far from proscribing Catholic universities, calls for them and requires them. As a matter of fact, a pluralistic society cannot exist unless each conviction, each *Weltanschauung*, is allowed to express itself and unfold there freely, together with its own institutions. Precisely because the world is pluralistic, it needs Catholic universities to train men of competence and conviction who can bring to a pluralistic society the authentic values implied in their conception of the world. The same holds true for that form of pluralism called ecumenism. There can be no worthwhile ecumenism without qualified interlocutors who are all the better suited to initiate a dialogue in proportion as they know what they are talking about and appreciate the values at issue. Again, it is the Catholic university—firm in its convictions but open to divergent positions—which can best form such interlocutors.

An Open World

As we have already said, no one can tell exactly what the world of tomorrow will be like. In a certain sense, anything is possible. Never in the history of mankind, surely, has a situation been so wide open as that in which we are living. Man has cast off the habits of centuries and even millennia. Science and technology place almost limitless possibilities at his disposal, up to and including the possibility of his self-destruction. But let us not contemplate such a somber prospect. Trusting in man's will to survive and in the wholesome forces which it unceasingly elicits in his bosom, let us rather look toward the future and the rich possibilities that lie before us. Some foresee the emergence of a uniform society, composed of robots mercilessly manipulated by anonymous forces and reduced to the role of mere cogs in an immense, inhuman machine. This is how science fiction tends to portray the man of the future. Personally, I do not believe in such a deceptive vision. Instead, I believe that, impelled by his innate need of freedom, man will devise ways to escape gradually from the many conventions and determinisms which, so far, have hampered the full development of his potentialities.

Far be it from me to predict a sort of return to paradise; being what he is, man will always feel his limitations and always encounter obstacles. But, in my humble opinion, he will be called more and more to take his destiny in his own hands. Less and less will the young find ready-made careers awaiting them; the game will be too open for the various moves to be made in advance. There will be need of great plasticity, disponibility, a sense of initiative and responsibility in order to orient oneself and achieve complete self-fulfillment in a world with almost unlimited possibilities. That is why, starting now, our universities should strive to train men who, beyond inevitable specialization, have an open mind and possess a capacity for invention and adaptation which will allow them to cope with extremely fluid situations. This is the context in which, at the beginning of this article, I expressed reservations about vocational training as the aim of a university's activity. To be sure, a university has the duty to train students by teaching them what they need to know in their chosen profession. It is even normal that the State or another body—eventually the university itself—examine the curricula in order to guarantee, in the interests of society, an adequate preparation for these students. But a university cannot limit itself to that. It must develop in its students what Bergson called "un supplément d'âme", a quality which will enable them not to let themselves be immured within their specialty, however interesting and important it may be, but remain interested in all that is human. *Nihil humanum a me alienum puto.* The better we succeed in creating a more human world, the more it will be an open world and the more we shall need men with open minds and broad horizons. Catholic universities—because, by their nature, they awaken man to transcendence and to the whole of humanity—are singularly fitted to inculcate this open-mindedness in their members through theory and practice.

Conclusion

We have come to the end of our reflections on the subject, but, in a way, this is where we should begin. Nothing has been said, for instance, about the concrete contribution of Catholic universities to the training of students for the world of tomorrow. That would be an extremely interesting topic, indeed, but in order to discuss it at all adequately, we would have to be able to base our statements on surveys made in the principal Catholic universities—something which would require considerable spadework. Since I do not possess such information and since the editors have asked a philosopher to discuss this problem, I thought it would be better to take as the starting point of my reflections the very nature of the Catholic university. No doubt, someone could name individual Catholic universities which do not correspond to the optimistic picture we have drawn. Unfortunately, human reality often falls short of what it could be. Despite these inevitable deficiencies, however, I can confidently say that the past and present record of our Catholic universities is proof of their efficacious contribution to the building of tomorrow's world. To the pessimists, who do not (or who no longer) believe in the Catholic university as a valid institution in our actual world, I reply that the two Catholic universities which I know from personal experience—those of Louvain and Fribourg—have played and are now playing an important role in the formation of capable and competent men, convinced Christians, who have helped and are still helping positively to assure the presence of the Christian message in those areas where the ideas and institutions that will shape the world of tomorrow are themselves being shaped today. The more faithful our Catholic universities remain to their ideal, the more they will prove to be a decisive factor in the building of a more human world.

Henk Linnebank/*Brussels, Belgium*

Participation in Industrial Management

It is an established fact that the management structure in industry is being questioned by influential people who are not involved in the social dispute, particularly in the principal industrial countries of Western Europe.

This is happening, first of all, in France where this question persisted after the "events" of May and June last year, and where De Gaulle made some rather explicit promises when he proposed certain reforms. It is also happening in Germany where the powerful *Deutsche Gewerkschaftsbund* are pressing for the introduction of the plan passed by the occupying powers for the coal and steel industry in the decree of 1951, a plan affecting about 400 other major industries that are dependent upon those products. It is happening in the same way in Holland where an official commission under the direction of Professor Verdam produced a report two years ago; this served as a basis for concrete proposals made by a commission for the extension of the powers of industrial councils, to be set up by the Council for Social Economy. In Belgium and England, too, the question is hotly debated, although not in the official meetings between employers and employees.

The discussion starts usually in university circles and occasionally in the trade unions. The challenge is then taken up by

43

the authorities and the employers' organizations. The latter are beginning to realize the truth of the slogan that appeared in January 1968 on the front page of the journal (printed in French) of the Belgian Christian employers: "Subir ou créer l'avenir?" ("Must we undergo or create the future?")

The unification of Europe has not yet reached the stage where it is possible to produce a comparative analysis of the situation in the major countries. An *Aufsichtsrat,* a *Conseil d'Administration,* a College of Commissioners and a Board of Directors are four rather different things which defy a single translation. The *Vorstand,* the Council of Directors, the Managing Board, the Council of Management and the *Comité de Direction* all represent the day-to-day management, but powers and limitations vary from one country to another. And yet, acquaintance with the varying scales of values that prevail in the different countries of Western Europe and knowledge of the corresponding positions of authority would be very useful if we want to overcome the difficulties created by these language barriers. To give a small example: politically, the French may be considered more articulate and more mature than the Germans, but France is sociologically still quite clearly an agrarian country, while West Germany is already an industrial one. We like to amuse ourselves about the autocratic military command structures which have rather easily been taken as typical of the Germans from Bismarck to Hitler. What is less commonly realized is that the influence of Napoleon is still very much kept alive by De Gaulle in the French "President-Director-General" and that his authority arouses the envy of many a Prussian *Junker* and officer.

It is true that a number of factors are bringing the European countries so close together that what happens in one country—for instance, in the field of co-responsibility—has immediate repercussions in a whole series of other countries, even if only by stimulating the discussion. Among these factors the Treaty of Rome and Servan Schreiber's *Défi Américain* ("American challenge") are certainly prominent.

In what follows I shall indicate some facts and concrete situations, together with some analyses, and finally present a "committed" approach to the question of the employers.

Fact and Situations

The Treaty of Rome, which aimed at opening up the markets of the participating States to all—though at the moment mainly the industrial—members, was more quickly and better understood by the Americans than by the partners to the treaty themselves.

The industrial cooperation which immediately began to flourish usually led to agreements between European and American industries, for the Americans very quickly saw the immediate advantages of a vast market with great purchasing power and hastened to make a number of European businessmen "happy" by offering generous conditions for mergers. This kind of activity continued for a considerable time until the editor-in-chief of the French L'Express put together a number of facts, well known in professional circles, in such a blunt journalistic manner that a reaction set in; as a result, today inter-European cooperation is beginning to assume a definite shape.

This is important for our subject because the reconversions which resulted from these upheavals began to touch the European workers and employees who, in the meantime, had grown accustomed to decent food, housing and motorcars.

These shocking attempts at the setting up of vast production organizations, adjusted to the situation in the European market, made the labor force and their trade union leaders wake up to the fact that large concentrations of power were being set up above and without them, which decided not only their chances of finding work but their whole security for the future as working human beings. Even when they admitted that the employers accepted these mergers with the best of intentions and often out of necessity, they realized—often for the first time—that they would have to become involved so that their interests would be protected when mergers were being discussed.

Therefore, it was really the growth of the European economic community and the changes in the structures of the European production system resulting from it which made the workers realize the importance of having a greater say in the process.

Their leaders, particularly those of Christian background, had already had this point on their list of desiderata for a long time, but they had shelved it for lack of response from the vast majority of their members. Socialist trade unionists had been more interested in control from the top through official or semi-official authoritative bodies.

The interest taken by Christian trade unionists in co-responsibility in the direction and management of business has always been cautious and rarely enthusiastic. This was partly because they were unable to present a clear new image in which the trade union movement itself could play a relatively important part and because they thus exposed themselves to a criticism which they found it hard to tolerate since, with a few exceptions, it was unjust—namely the reproach that they were aiming at more power for themselves. That is why until quite recently the protagonists of more democratic structures in industry were found mainly in university circles.

And thus, 100 years after the utopians and industrial ideologists first dared mention the basic lines of thought, co-responsibility in Western Europe did not get any further than industrial councils, representative bodies chosen by the employees with a certain right to information and discussion about the economic course of business, with some advisory rights about social matters.

Analyses

The setting up of these industrial councils was a laborious affair in most Western European countries. And this is certainly not exclusively the fault of the employers, as is so often and so gleefully asserted. The most important factor in this problem lies, for better or for worse, with the degree of *general* education among those who work in industry, from top to bottom —employers, trained executives and workers.

From long and daily experience I know of many cases where employers, often quite competent in business, genuinely wanted to set up a fairly viable industrial council but found their good will smothered in the indifference of the workers and the ill will of the intermediate sector, and so saw themselves in the role of the servant whose debt was forgiven by the Lord. They indeed often lacked the formation or the gift to bridge the gaps created in human relationships by a century of purely functional thinking. And those who could do so—industrial advisers, sociologists, psychologists, etc.—often lack the businessman's ability to see to it that the wheels keep turning and that orders will come in, and this reduces the credibility of their advice.

The businessman who, convinced by the facts of the situation, is prepared to introduce the structural changes required by modern society is in fact faced today with great difficulties. The number of such businessmen who genuinely want to do this is larger than people know, while the little progress they make is too easily seen as ill will. A description of the factors which influence this process would fill a library.

Many businessmen have long been convinced of the justice of the demand for a greater say and more control on the part of those whose personal life is linked with the industry. What they do not see—and this is also the case of many representatives of the intelligentsia or the unions—is simply how the excellent principles, often formulated in such a masterly manner by the social reformers, can be translated into structures that are viable in practice without a too explicit intervention by lawmakers.

Moreover, here and there there is still a lack of basic connection between university training and industrial life, although useful contacts between these two spheres have given rise to violent reactions on the part of the students who want to prevent a financial marriage between capital and science. Constructive, free and democratic slum-clearing is therefore indispensable to the solution of the communication problem in industry when a bridge between labor and management has to be built.

An argument against co-responsibility, still frequently heard in employers' circles, is that until recently employees have been far more interested in achieving a whole series of other goals than in co-responsibility. But their genuinely worried leaders, while not denying the truth of this assertion, regard this as a primary proof that co-responsibility is absolutely essential.

This leads to the essential issue in tackling this problem. Who must exercise this share in responsibility—the workers, the unions, or, to start with, the intermediate sector of trained executives?

How Do We Build Up This Co-Responsibility?

The question of who should exercise this co-responsibility is an historically controversial issue on which little light has been cast by either businessmen or trade unions. In general one may say that the businessmen usually take the line that they will not accept interference in the economic course of their industry by the union because they consider the union as an "alien intrusion" in the industry as a whole.

Particularly in Anglo-Saxon countries, but also elsewhere, they accept a representative, chosen by the workers, who is free to function in the factory as the contact man with the union. However, the law on industrial organization (*Betriebsverfassungsgesetz*) in Germany and laws governing industrial councils have given the unions the right to propose their candidate, and so the principle has evaporated. But there are still very many employers who would be prepared, in a spirit of industrial community sense, to share more information with their own workers than with the union leaders who are not working in their firm.

Here, too, the question of training plays an important part. This training—which I am convinced is a linear function that must foster participation—is often seen as the problem of the low level of education on the part of the workers. But looking at it objectively, we see that all those involved, labor leaders included, need this more detailed training.

Such training is an important item for the dialogue between employers and employees, both in the actual industry and in their own organizations. This so-called training activity is a controversial issue both among employers and unionists, and was often debated during the years of decline. Usually one board member is delegated to handle this particular item, and he speaks so convincingly about this being the very nerve of the organization's existence that everybody agrees and the budgetary item is safe for another year. The difficulty in this work is that one should clearly define the aim of this training in an age when change and renewal are the order of the day.

Training for conscious membership in an economic industrial community can never be given completely outside this community. Theoretical know-how is not the same as living practice, unless it is part of the psychosociological context of the formal and informal group structures of the actual industry. That is why the growth toward new structures is a process which must involve in the first place the employer himself, his staff and all his employees together. *All* those involved must experience the new relationships as *their own*. None of the parties must feel the new elements as imposed or extorted. This can only happen if all have been able to take an active part in the shaping of those elements. In the case of "open" companies it should not be unthinkable for the shareholders to also be invited to take part in the discussion, so that workers can hear the point of view of those who provide the capital. The capitalist system is often, and rightly—but also rather glibly—criticized. The way to change it into a more human system must be a human way, and here such discussions would be invaluable.

From the point of view of organization, both employers and employees should see to it that the training is far more integrated. Occasionally trade union leaders are invited to introduce an employers' seminar for modern industrial management and vice versa, and sometimes the name of an employer or personnel manager figures in the program of a trade union course, but so far it is all still a rather reluctant business.

It is rather ridiculous and even futile that in both camps the members tell each other how to deal with representatives of the other camp. It seems to me that both the trade union movement and the employers' organizations could and should play a far more important part in the collective and mutual training for co-responsibility.

By playing a more active part in this "long and laborious" process, the trade union movement could exercise far more influence on the course of events than is believed possible—more, in any case, than by forcing a labor director or labor commissioners on the employers. This does not mean that the ultimate result may not appear to lie in that direction, but the question is how such a decision will be reached: by conflict or by cooperation. And in this actual dilemma I opt, with firm conviction, for cooperation, not only for psychological and sociological reasons but also for political ones.

Hermann Wallraff, S.J./*Frankfurt, West Germany*

Worker Participation in Decision-Making and Management

Worker participation in manage-ment means that employee repre-sentatives would have a say in the basic economic decisions of the factory, the business enterprise and the national economy. Debate over this whole question is not a new issue. The specifics of the notion have become more concrete with the passage of decades, but the basic notion itself has been argued back and forth for many generations, and the argument is still going on. Similar ideas and movements have cropped up in other sectors of societal life, and they have spread, in one form or another, to many lands.

Worker Participation and Emancipation Movements

When we compare the issue of participatory management with similar movements in recent social history, we can hardly call it a bold gamble or a passing fad. Its opponents are mistaken in believing that they need only hold it at bay until the fad passes. There is strong evidence that this desire for participation in decision-making and management is a continuation of the general thrust toward emancipation in the 18th and 19th centuries. In short, we are dealing with a trend that has typified a lengthy period of time.

The concrete goals of workers have varied greatly from country to country, and from one epoch to the next. But they seem to

51

represent a common desire to overcome the economic and social setup that other classes hoped to fashion and institutionalize. This general aim is unmistakable, even though more concrete efforts were applied to the development of ever more effective unions. Employees often focused all their efforts on winning shorter hours and higher wages. But despite all their progress, they remained aware of the fact that they were protesting against a form of economic dictatorship that generally favored the capitalist or his spokesman.

The many protective laws passed in favor of the worker by national governments were meant to make the workers a participating subject in economic decisions, not just a beneficiary of monetary aid. After the great world depressions and two world wars, full employment became an obligatory plank in every political platform. A concomitant result was to organize the political economy in such a way that the bargaining power of employees would be as large as possible. Greater worker participation was also the aim of numerous political programs designed to spread private property (as capital goods) on a broader base. Long ago Rousseau pointed to the social necessity of integrating private property with the law of equality, but this effort has not proved very successful.

In reality, the carefully planned booms of the second half of the 20th century have intensified the class-structured conglomeration of productive private capital. The conflict has been softened only insofar as political championing of private property has led to political programs designed to make this a widespread reality. The dominance of the propertied classes has been neutralized in that many parties have now become owners of property themselves. The old conflict has become less acute, but it has not been fully resolved.

From the start, the workers' representatives have pointed out that day-to-day labor contributes much to the success of a business enterprise. Property itself is not the only important contribution. Even though the workers may have their share of private property, they are still workers in the plant, not its owners, and they want to have a say there also. That has been one of their perduring demands.

Now this demand is not an arbitrary one. It stems from the belief, underlined in *Mater et Magistra,* that work is one of the most direct expressions of man's nature and, as such, is more precious than an abundance of external goods. Under a wide variety of names and institutional forms, this claim has been advanced in all industrial cultures, and it is still a worldwide trend. The fact that an ever larger number of workers are enjoying material prosperity has heightened rather than dampened their desire for participatory management. As they have progressed up the scale of prosperity, they have become more keenly aware of their own position in society.

Many workers are better provided for than the lower echelons of self-supporting and self-employed people. Their social prestige grows in proportion to the luxuries they can afford. By virtue of their vocational training and studies in regular schools and trade schools, they are at least as well educated as the average capitalist. It is a simple fact that the amazing stability of our present political system is due, in no small measure, to the mature attitude of the country's workers. They have contributed as much as any other group to the rebuilding of our economy, both as individuals and as an organized bloc.

All this is not lost on the worker. It heightens his self-awareness and makes him feel all the more that his lack of participation in the decision-making process is not acceptable in the contemporary situation. Workers want to erase this last vestige of a bygone age, insofar as it can be done. Their desire for a change has become a political program for other strong factions in society; thus it hardly seems likely that their expectations can be blocked much longer.

In Great Britain, France, Italy and Austria, workers pursue the same goal under different slogans, for in these countries the concerned enterprises are wholly withdrawn from the influence that private property usually exerts. As a result, the unions pursue their demand for participatory management directly or indirectly through the available political channels. They try to ensure a voice in political decisions which, in West Germany, are the province of specific corporate bodies. The labor unions in these countries, unlike their German counterparts, are political organs.

In the Communist world, the same basic problem has been solved quite differently. Because of the underlying ideology, private capital was not only ousted as the central factor in production, but it was, for all practical purposes, abolished. The overriding role of private property, as evidenced by history, was not neutralized by socialization or counterbalancing participation; it was replaced by a one-sided determination, supposedly made in the name of the working class. The net result has been a bureaucracy, now sharply criticized by young people and the intelligentsia. Their criticism echoes the general desire for participation that is typical of our present era.

Developments in other areas of societal life support our contention that there is a general desire to participate in the decision-making process. The unrest of youths and students all over the world may take questionable forms at times, but it clearly demonstrates that they are no longer willing to be the passive object of decisions made by others. In family life, the last vestiges of patriarchal control are coming under critical scrutiny. Even the Catholic Church has been caught up in this movement. Laymen want to be heard by the clergy; parochial priests want to have a say in the selection of their bishops and in the progress of their dioceses. Everywhere a functional concept of authority is replacing the older notion of self-sufficient authority. The ear of authority is to listen to the spokesmen of those it rules.

Opposing Arguments and Their Weaknesses

In whatever sector of society this new trend has appeared, and no matter what concrete forms it has taken, it has been accompanied by opposition and conflict. It is not surprising, then, that the demand for participatory management should meet with continuing and determined resistance. And the opposing view is quite capable of posing high-sounding and seemingly reasonable objections.

All ideas and institutions can be misused and abused, so the abstract possibility of such abuse is not a convincing argument in itself. Yet some opponents of participatory management do not hesitate to challenge this idea by alluding to this possibility. For them, the abstract possibility itself is enough to point up the absurdity of the whole idea. When it comes to talk about private capital, on the other hand, these same people want to talk about concrete cases rather than vaguely possible abuses. Some academicians, for example, point to the possibility of a large business being ruined by the incompetence or maliciousness of workers who had a say in its management. This extreme case (and a hypothetical one at that!) is presented as a conclusive argument against any concrete program of participatory management.

Now a person can fashion innumerable arguments of this sort. But if they are not based on sober sociological analysis, which deals with concrete realities and concrete human behavior, they do not have anything to offer toward the solution of this question. They can only appeal to people who are not interested in scrutinizing the pros and cons of the issue. Moreover, there is always a great deal of resistance to new ideas that have not yet been tried out in practice or stood the test of time. Their potential dangers weigh more heavily on people's minds, especially when people have had enough experiments.

The debate over various forms of participatory management is handicapped by the fact that many people are reluctant to make necessary distinctions. Arguments, which logically apply only to one or two specific forms of participation, are used to challenge the whole idea of participation and to turn people's minds against it. Some critics, for example, give the impression that any and every form of worker participation would involve the danger of radical syndicalism—i.e., that the workers and trade unions would take control of society and the means of production.

Now the fact is that the participatory process already implemented in the German mining industry is not under the exclusive control of the trade unions. The controlling body of the industry is composed of eleven members. Five members are representatives of the employees. Two of these five representatives are elected by the employees, and they themselves must be employees; two are representatives of the interested trade unions; the fifth employee representative is not to be an employee or a trade-union member.

In actual practice, lines have not formed according to the setup outlined above. Experience indicates that the participating members, whether they are union members or not, do not parrot union demands when they take part in decisions of the board of directors. It is easy to see why this should be so, on sociological grounds. The duties and problems of a board of directors are quite different from those of a trade union, so there is a safe distance between the two functions. The trade unions have not exercised central control over the participatory process, and it is unlikely that they ever will.

All the same, we would be flying in the face of sound principles if we allowed room for the participatory process to snowball into a concentrated pressure group. Insofar as it is possible, the process should be so set up that the individual participants are independent of one another and not associated with one and the same central body. Moreover, since the legitimate interests of a union representative differ from the interests and duties of a company board member, it is very difficult for one person to have to represent both viewpoints. In such a case, he is likely to opt for one side on most occasions.

To preclude this danger, it is preferable that there not be a preponderance of union members or union officials in the participatory process. Now this does not mean that we should exclude union representatives entirely from the board of directors. So long as the unions are the most effective representatives of the employees, we would be discriminating against the latter if we refused to let them be represented by union men on the board of directors.

Sometimes the participatory process may operate at a different level, outside the board of directors, particularly if the business is set up with two poles of influence and authority. In such a case, the employees may have as many representatives at company meetings as the stockholders do, but the individual employee does not exercise participatory management. Some people even argue that in such a setup the individual worker really doesn't participate in decisions at all. As they would have it, the whole process merely serves the interests of an elite group; it is just that the composition of this group has changed somewhat.

At first glance, this objection may seem quite plausible, but in reality it fails to comprehend the structure of every large society whose government is based on the principle of the consent of the governed. If this principle is to be preserved, if it is not to be replaced by monarchial or aristocratic rule, there just has to be *representative* government. The same holds true for any large business where the number of stockholders exceeds the number of seats on the board of directors.

To be sure, the relationship between the representatives and the represented is often poorly defined—both in theory and in practice—in many sectors of societal life. But the situation still seems preferable to authoritarian alternatives, and representation of all those involved is better than representation of only one party. This is what participatory management seeks to provide. Those who reject it for its lack of *adequate* representation are arguing a bit dishonestly, unless they openly espouse individual or group-centered responsibility.

If we compare a participatory management system (where the workers are represented by spokesmen) with a patriarchal setup (where only the shareholders have a say), then it becomes obvious that the situation of the individual worker is quite different in the former setup. Because his representatives do have a say in the decision-making process, the worker's interests are taken into consideration. They play a part in the operation of the business, and there is no small merit in that.

Some venture the objection that any and every form of participatory management is legally and ethically against the whole system of private property (as capital goods). But this objection does not hold up under critical analysis. If the participatory management process in the German mining industry violated basic property rights, the issue would have been taken to court long ago. The fact is that this particular process is quite compatible with a legally protected system of private capital, and so are similar schemes for participatory management.

If the process of participatory management is extended to other large industries, some corrections may have to be made to safeguard the legal rights of all concerned. But if the basic standards of the mining settlement are maintained, there is no reason why the interests of private capital should be hurt. If any interests had been damaged by the management system in the mining industry, the lawsuits would have been on the docket long ago. From the viewpoint of legitimate property rights, the details of a participatory scheme may have to be worked out very carefully, but a definite yes or no cannot be formulated on this basis alone.

Property Rights and Participatory Management

The law of property rights does not give the owner exclusive claim to decision-making in the operation of a business. The business property belongs to him alone, of course, and he can dispose of it as he sees fit. But other people take part in the actual operation of the business, and they have a right to stipulate the terms under which they will lend their cooperation. The right to participate in operational decisions can be one of these terms.

In many instances, the owners of a business have had to surrender authority that was properly theirs to outsiders. Banks, credit institutions, creditors and professional managers have made such demands on them. If these people are entitled to a say in the management of a business, it is difficult to deny the same right to employees who are even more personally involved in the business.

Another objection skirts the borderline between functional considerations and the ethics of private property. It maintains that participatory management subverts the efficiency coefficient that operates in the sphere of private capital. Under ordinary circumstances, it claims, the law of supply and demand and healthy competition will ensure that the interests of all will be protected. Now one may well envision a utopian system of private capital where the wishes of all people are safeguarded in the economy. But the reality is quite a different story, for there must be counterbalancing forces. Any sober sociological analysis of the average capitalist's behavior will reveal that he tends to denigrate and dominate those who are in an inferior economic position.

Functional Problems

The debate over participatory management has shifted to functional issues in many respects, and some arguments tend to crop up time and again. Participatory management, it is claimed, will necessarily hurt the flexibility of the business enterprise. The underlying presupposition often is that participatory management seeks to turn the business organization into a parliamentary setup, even though every concrete program of participatory management indicates that this is not so.

If we set this absurd presupposition aside, we can allay any remaining fears by stipulating certain basic ground rules: in a system of participatory management, no one has a right to interfere with the executive management in its day-to-day decisions; the board of directors is to consider only basic issues and policies, and it is not to be set up or operated in an atmosphere of class conflict. With these principles in effect, there is no reason why participatory management should adversely affect the flexibility of a business enterprise. The objection is a bugaboo.

The same can be said for the argument that incompetents might take over key positions. The process of participatory management should not be compared with an ideal and imaginary board of directors, but with the average board of directors. There, too, we find honorary posts, sinecures and unqualified members. The working class, moreover, with a total manpower that is five times as great as that of the capitalist class, should have a correspondingly larger reservoir of competent people.

This danger can be precluded by setting up certain qualification standards, for both sides. Behind this objection lies a deep-rooted presupposition that has often come to light in history: "The other fellows cannot do the job as well as we can." It is hard to argue rationally against this *a priori* position, as the history of every emancipation movement proves.

Another objection maintains that any and every form of participatory management will hurt the capital structure of the business enterprise—in particular, the influx of foreign investment. Now this argument just does not look at the facts. As far as we know, the participatory system in the German mining industry has not adversely affected capital participation and investment at home or from abroad. There seems to be no solid grounds to this objection. It is a dire but unfulfilled prophecy.

It is absolutely necessary that the whole question of participatory management be discussed objectively. Sound arguments and functional considerations must be given due examination, and we have only touched upon a few points in this article. In the last analysis, most people approach the question with their own set of value judgments. They defend the status quo because they prefer a particular model of society and its economic structures. The working class cherishes a different model of society, and it resents arbitrary presuppositions about its lack of competence and ability.

Since both sides approach the practical issues with such differing view points, it is not surprising that they reach different conclusions. The basic lines of this debate were formed long ago, and they have persisted throughout the whole emancipation process. But can there be any doubt about the final outcome?

Franciscus Tellegen/*Aalst, Netherlands*

The Responsible Development of Technology

The new technology, linked with physics, has produced instruments that are not only automatic but can also control themselves. They are productive systems, and it is natural to think of a productive enterprise as a system made up of men and means and aiming at self-maintenance.[1] Production presupposes consumption, and society can be described as a structure or (regulating) system of production and consumption in which these two constantly determine each other. Karl Marx foresaw and commended the new social structure of "labor and leisure".[2] H. Arendt has interpreted European history as leading to a society wholly dominated by the production-consumption process.[3]

Two Kinds of Problems

It is gradually becoming clear that this is only one of the ways in which we can cope with the new possibilities. The problems which inauguate technology, in the broad sense of the word, are of two kinds. On the one hand, man is passing from the situation

[1] Cf. K. Tuchel, *Herausforderung der Technik* (Bremen, 1967).

[2] Karl Marx, *Das Kapital* (Krönerausgabe, 1929), p. 317.

[3] H. Arendt, *The Human Condition* (New York, 1959): "It is quite conceivable that the modern age—which began with such an unprecedented and promising outburst of human activity—may end in the deadliest, most sterile passivity history has ever known" (p. 295).

in which labor as such is the basic condition of life to a new situation in which the choice of one possibility rather than another becomes the basic condition. This is the problem of affluence. On the other hand, the apparently inexorable progress of technology—seen as an actual reality—raises the question under which conditions the systematic organization of the provision of needs and the satisfaction of desires is salutary for the people involved. Technology is and remains essentially a means; it is a mediating agent between man and his environment, between man and man. As a scientific process it has not only broken down this barrier but has also become one of the determining factors of a new culture,[4] a new form of social life on this earth.

These two kinds of problems, the obverse and reverse of the same coin, find expression in the micro- and macro-forms of society, in the family and in politics. And here labor and leisure meet—concretely in the family and more conditionally in politics. Between these two lies the domain of the "free" public life. This article is an attempt to illustrate with a few examples the problems in these three fields.

The change in both the traditional and the now prevailing relationships between people is constantly encouraged today by the *means of information,* which are all based on technological invention. What was formerly reserved to a few is now absorbed in the life of many; they are all getting acquainted with other worlds and other views of life. All can now follow the discussion of burning topics and be informed about what happens elsewhere, although naturally in a different way from those immediately involved. The image or picture gradually assumes the same value as the word, and this creates more technological possibilities in the process. Slowly we are acquiring the insight necessary for making the best use of them. This can hardly be otherwise when we develop this insight experimentally. On this point the growing use of the instrument implies a "cultural lag" in both the

---

[4] C. J. Dippel and J. M. de Jong, *Geloof en natuurwetenschap* (The Hague, 1965). Dippel speaks of technology as a cultural force without autonomy (p. 278).

"producers" and the "consumers". But this also implies from the very start the problem of finding norms. In brief, what fosters communication between people? Those to whom the programs are directed must be able to express their reaction to the choice made by the programmers, and this reaction must be effective if there is to be communication at all. It seems to me that here those with a scientific training may not systematically limit their contribution to their professional knowledge, although this remains the first thing required of them; their share in responsibility must extend to the problem as a whole which is the concern of all.

One field where the modern sense of responsibility of those with a scientific training is only beginning to penetrate is that of *scientific education,* where teaching must be linked to research. The rise of audio-visual aids and machines required for entry into one sector of the profession is breaking through the monopoly of the spoken word and may be compared to the search for standardized tests. Pressed, and occasionally forced, by the students, lecturers have begun to examine themselves critically and this examination has led to the question of the relevancy of the present ways of transmitting knowledge and of assessment, and even beyond—under the slogan of "the critical university". The point here is precisely the social responsibility of those already educated, and this implies more than the responsibility inherent in the practice or exercise of acquired professional ability. An institution of scientific education cannot reject the effective promotion of such social responsibility. For such a rejection is linked with a view of science that has become out-of-date and would in fact encourage the continuation of the existing structures and distribution of power. A systematic approach to humanly purposeful activity in view of practical reality is required here, together with the awareness that such a systematic approach is not the ultimate but the penultimate end. The working system must remain subordinate to the ends of man. Its use must therefore remain subject to critical judgment, and its development must be guided.

Objectively functioning regulations and systematized provisions have played an historically important part in the emancipation of the workers by way of *politics*. Originally directed toward the relief of various needs such as illness, accidents, housing and education, they broadened out gradually until they embraced the fulfillment of the justified wishes of all. This is clear in the planning of "new town" projects. Today the housing of a community embraces all people, and the basic criterion for the "new town" is easy access for all to places of work and recreation. In the concern with human needs we notice a comparable broadening of purpose in the prevention of needs by the creation of new possibilities. Regulations of a social and political character, aimed at groups of needy people of various kinds, are supplemented by initiatives that spring from society itself and clearly envisage the individual. And so a systematic whole is being built in which, politically speaking, found provisional expression in the laws about social security through which those who are in need have the "right" to "claim" assistance from the authorities. The tendency is to create a system of care which will guarantee to all a minimal livelihood and qualified assistance. By and large one can agree with this "development", but at the same time one wonders, technically speaking, whether such a regulation does not in fact again accept the existing social structure. Is it not possible that, because of its structure, this society generates people in need of assistance? Does the voice of those who appeal, possibly strengthened by those who have scientifically analyzed the situation, count in working out any further "development"? Here, too, the cooperation of those who are scientifically trained should go beyond their merely professional contribution to a "set" problem.

Technology has enabled man to produce means of destruction that are effective beyond human imagining. They have been developed and are still being further developed. The question of war or peace has become the principal issue in politics and will probably remain so for some time. Here the development is leading to automatic instruments by which someone sets the programmed process of destruction going. It is clear that this abolishes the centuries-old question of a "just war". Instead, we have now the positive calculation of escalation or de-escalation, as well as the new question about a "just revolution" (including violence) which is exclusively related to an attack on the power-structure that prevents such a development. At the moment the problem of preventing war is tied up with the problem of development: How will the so-called developed countries give other countries the genuine chance of sharing in this "developed" situation? One can suggest that many so-called developing countries function as the laboratories where the developed countries test their theories about an effective coping with "development" on a technological basis.[5] There are other suggestions, some worse, some better, than this one. But if this suggestion is accepted, it will at least have the advantage of providing a genuine and viable basis for "cooperation" in development. The implicit presupposition must then be made explicit—namely, that developed countries only share in an event insofar as this is an event common to all. Only by all pulling together can we hope to get this "development" with all its implications under control. The very urgency of it unites all. Here, too, the fact that those scientifically trained must be concerned with practical realities is indispensable, but not enough. For it is here a matter of manipulating scientific development itself.

Even in the smallest circle of people—the living together for the sake of life itself—the relationship between the partners is undergoing a drastic change due to technology. Physical and biological research has given man the power to disentangle the sexual experience from procreation, the continuation of the species. And we can look forward to further developments: the determination of sex and the power to influence heredity, among other things. Thus mankind is assuming power over its own continuity in a way that was unthinkable in the past, and every human being is confronted with those new possibilities in a concrete

[5] Cf. W. E. Moore, *The Impact of Industry* (Englewood Cliffs, 1965).

way. Responsible treatment of sexuality can no longer be tied up with procreation as was the case in the past. This is more prominent in the present interest in sex than the attempt to build up a new ethics in the field. There is good reason to expect new initiatives here, particularly on the part of woman, for she will decide in this new situation whether intercourse with a man will lead to conception or not.

The Search for an Ethics of Development

I have repeatedly used the word "development", even in the title. The term is used here only in connection with human activity, and I introduced it in the description of the new technology. In its most obvious social expression—industrialization—development lies between research and production. Development is the bridge from new knowledge to the organization of new working methods. In itself, development is neither knowledge nor manufacture for production, but rather the interaction between the two. The development of results born of research consists in finding new practical applications for practical life and testing them by their viability. Active development is typified by technical creativity, the discovery of ways and means by which progressive knowledge can be made to lead to new and effective working methods.

As L. W. Nauta has rightly observed,[6] the term "project" can also be used to describe the link between knowing and making. However, I prefer the term "development" because it directly expresses the purpose of this activity. But it is true that development is worked out in the form of projects. As the key word for the new ethics involved in this, J. Fourastié has introduced the term "option" (a deliberately chosen preference).[7] Development, project and option have this in common: they are all concerned with the link between knowing and making, and they comprise both factuality and possibility. There remains room for

[6] L. W. Nauta, *Jean-Paul Sartre* (Baarn, 1966), p. 111.
[7] J. Fourastié, *Essais de morale prospective; vers une nouvelle morale* (Paris, 1967).

change on the basis of science or experience. My objection to "option" is that its connotation is so subjective that it cannot express an event as objectively experienced, and this is what we need in the present situation.

Thus we take "development" here as the hallmark of the new technology. For, like science, this is a self-developing process, in contrast with handwork which cannot be reduced to a "natural process". This character of the new technology disentangles "development" from the succession of generations. To choose scientific training means therefore to choose a profession or career which demands permanent participation in scientific (including technological) development.

This cultivation of working method and instrument therefore stretches well beyond factory production. The connection between the satisfaction of needs and the fulfillment of desire in man demands constant widening. Wherever human purposes and means to achieve them can be distinguished, and wherever the means can be formulated in the scientific description of processes, technology comes in. And so "development" is viable as a key word, both for the objective description of this historical phase and for the responsible creation of new possibilities in practical life.

This learning to live with constantly changing and increasing possibilities, with the necessity of choosing and of modifying the choice on the ground of experience, implies a rejection of the traditional ethic and the search for a new one. At the moment the first is rather more prominent than the second. In many ways it is being made clear that man feels himself threatened by being reduced to a tool, in small issues as in large ones, not only by the existing establishment, but also by the systematic imposition of that establishment, and this without a chance of escape. Borderline cases illustrating this rejection spring up like mushrooms all over the world. This is understandable in a situation where every ethic which takes its norms from one or other predetermined "natural" order has lost its validity. An equally systematic orientation will now have to be methodically worked out, tending toward free human participation, evoked by the existing situation and responded to by those who are involved in it. As human persons we shall have to discover ourselves how we can cope responsibly with the new possibilities. Here the small group, living together, has a primary part to play. This can only become fruitful when people, possibly in groups, are systematically involved in the development of social institutions—enterprises, schools, cultural life, town planning, etc.—right up to the political level, because it is there that decisions are taken about the scope and priorities of measures that will in great part determine the future. We are living *in* a "given" development, and this is only humanly possible when we are living *with* development—i.e., can steer it toward deliberately chosen aims and do so on the basis of new insights and new experiences.[8]

Let me illustrate this with a small-scale and a large-scale example. The mutually agreed decision to continue as partners in life—an alternative to the traditional forms of entering upon a matrimonial alliance—can, ethically speaking, be formulated in terms of development. A first acquaintance, in whatever connection, can develop into looking for each other, an exchange of feelings and thoughts in many ways. In such a context the biological term "growth" (development) is not the only one that is applicable, but there is a conscious effort toward a mutual and living empathy, not so much as a factual datum but above all as an actual possibility, in terms of a man in search of himself. To continue as partners in life in a responsible manner cannot rest principally on what is already given, but should be based on expectation, on the development of mutual trust, so that in the development of the partnership the two people involved become more themselves. When we see the situation in this light, such questions as carnal intercourse before marriage and the appearance of the first child are no longer *a priori* the first questions to consider. These are questions which will confront those who

---

[8] A clear example of this in the field of international development activity is given by Barbara Ward in *The Decade of Development—A Study in Frustration?* (London, 1966).

marry and to which there is no simple answer for everyone—
certainly not for the time being. To act responsibly in an ethical
sense is to act in a way in which the action can fulfill a rational
function within a development.

For the example on a large scale I would point to the interaction between industrial life and other social institutions. It seems
clear to me that in industrial life we can find examples not only
of built-in development with regard to product and working
method, but also of development in connection with social relationships (the structure of authority) and the cultural aspects
(the shaping of the industry). Moreover, there are many instances which show that the criteria for an enterprise are affected
by changes in other social institutions, such as hospitals, schools,
offices and churches, etc.

The point here is not to transform all institutions into enterprises, nor the unquestioned acceptance of the actual situation in
industry. The old truth that only few people are necessary in
order to bring about the cooperation of many remains valid.
Forms of this, in which the participation of many is put to opti-
mal use, should at least include the participation of those
involved in decision-making and also the responsibility of
answering for the decisions taken to those involved, as far as possible. The meaning of "capable direction" and "strong management" will vary according to the individual case. The context of
such interaction implies that social and cultural provisions must
rest on an acceptable economic basis, and that industrial life,
seen as a typically economic provision, must embody social and
cultural aspects in its aims. This seems to me a large-scale example of a development ethic today.

The large, average and small instances of this ethic cannot
proceed independently. For the development of this ethic it is
important to realize that it is just as important to tackle it on a
small scale as on a large one. Structural reforms do not necessarily precede changes in the dispositions of people. They should
go hand in hand, something that will apparently always remain a
difficult process for us as human beings. This is proved by the

students' demand for a repeat of the 19th-century workers' revolution. Questions about such issues as the ethical justification of a revolution and the use of violence can only be answered from within the ethic of development.

How To Be a Christian in This Period of Transition

The actual cultural transition is characterized by a revolution in man's freedom and restraint, and in his relations with others and with the world. The new freedom consists in the (possible) lapse of "natural" impositions, of a situation where man is tied to nature seen as fixed in the existing environment and the existing body, and this includes inter-human relations that were formerly considered to be "natural". The possibility to go one's own way, to plan or develop one's personal life, never imagined in the past, is now thrown open, at both the individual and communal level. The new restraint lies in the definite cultivation of systematized provisions and in the necessity to direct this development, personally and together. We must constantly prevent the few from seizing power over the many. The way to do this must constantly be sought and developed experimentally. The dialectic interaction of freedom and restraint remains, but it will now tend toward freedom of choice, always coupled to the fact that choose we must. Human life is becoming detached from a predetermined cosmos within which freedom and restraint operate. It is now turning toward life and life together, toward the future and toward a world that is habitable for all, and where what is given in nature is given its true meaning in the satisfaction of man's needs and the fulfillment of man's desires.

Christ's appearance in history and his message—in effect, one single event—are not done away with in this transition, but they must be newly formulated and understood afresh in the new cultural context, the new "perspective", for although in the Christian view this event could be expressed in the context of religions bound up with a static "nature" or "cosmos" or with particular cultures, these are far from exhausting it. This does not diminish the difficulty of the new understanding, and this difficulty can only be overcome through a dialogue among Christians who, in various ways, find themselves caught up in this transition. Second, we must find a point of contact from which this new formulation can start. It seems to me that this starting point lies embedded in the situation which is common to all—namely, that of living in this phase of transition. The question of how to cope with the development of constantly new possibilities on the basis of a praxis bound up with science, in small groups as well as large, dominates our actual life, both personal and communal. That question, which affects all people and all spheres of life, is a point of contact which lies there for the taking. It is obvious that the question of being a Christian cannot be reduced to the universal question which affects all, for that would dissolve the Christian question as such. We must constantly reexamine the interaction between "faith and order" and "life and work", starting from the basic point of contact. We are on our way toward a life and a world in the state of self-development, without ever being in a position to produce a blueprint. We can only discover the active presence of the Christian message when we start from this realization.

When thinking about how to translate what has been said into concrete terms, we can see two more specific points. It seems to me that Christians are groups of people who must actively foster the discovery of an adequate ethic in any set of historical circumstances. For every culture or cultural period is the expression of both an attitude to life and a view about what is ethically right or wrong in human conduct. The message of man's salvation, as understood by Christians, operates in all ages and for all peoples, and is therefore not itself an ethic locked up in history. The purpose of the message is to operate salvation, and the question is what this consists of today. In this actual attempt at finding the new ethic, the primary competence lies with the people of the Church, not with those who devote themselves to the Church as such. But this work cannot be done if it is not undertaken and critically enriched by a community of faithful, a Church. Church government, understood as service to such a community, is meant to keep the relation clear between message and work by preaching and celebrating. This shows the need for a constant and open dialogue within the Church, as well as the need to make the words credible through deeds. At the same time this shows the impossibility of clinging to forms of authority which were valid in other ages.

This change may be briefly illustrated by looking at the matter of preparation for and the practice of married life. In contrast with the past, the decision-taking in this field will be more and more the partners' own. The "getting to know each other" which must precede the decision to marry will have to be far more comprehensive as norms imposed from outside fall away. And so marriage, too, will bear the stamp of that general "development". Of this, the decision about the size of the family, with its medical, socio-psychological and cultural implications, is a part. It seems to me obvious that the Church's habit of prescribing a particular pattern of conduct—possibly valid in an earlier agrarian environment—is now out of date. The realization that the intending and actual partners are primarily themselves responsible here is a liberating experience, just as the abolition of an ecclesiastical administration side by side with civil registration. But this is not saying all that has to be said, although some would like to make us believe so. Christians cannot be satisfied with sharing in the active search for what this coping with new possibilities will mean. They will want to do this by starting from one or other idea about "marrying in Christ", taken not as a norm to be applied, but as an ideal. In this search the Lord will be in their midst and in his time open the eyes of those, married and unmarried, who seek *in Christ,* as what they seek becomes visible in their lives.

The second point which Christians must now also observe seems to me to consist in relativizing on principle all claims to absoluteness, which are so frequent in the world today. This implies a definite preference for negative border-situations, the perspective of life as a mere game, the appearance of "emancipated" man, and all such statements or attitudes. The far-reaching extent to which man's life, in joy as in sorrow, depends on "free gifts", on grace, reminds the Christian of his basic conviction, however inadequately translated into practice, that fundamentally man's personal and communal life does not depend on human insight and human labor, still less on fate or some cosmic process. It is taken up in an all-embracing "providence", in a grace which operates from creation to fulfillment and gives human existence its ultimate meaning. The travail of a new world, understood as contained within the context of human history, is for the faithful an appeal to their faith. This can preserve them from escaping from the world in which they live and from identifying themselves with it to such an extent that there is no longer any room for faith.

Rudolf Kautzky/*Hamburg, West Germany*

Scientific Progress and Ethical Problems in Modern Medicine

I

THE MANIPULATION OF HUMAN LIFE

As modern medicine progresses, the physician is gaining ever increasing control over the life of man. It can begin at the very start of a person's life and extend beyond its end. We all are familiar with the medical means of controlling birth (in both the positive and the negative sense), with experiments to influence genetic structures, and with medical treatment of the unborn child. It is now possible to remove large parts of the brain and most of the lower torso when this is medically indicated. The activity of the kidneys, heart and lungs can be sustained for years by mechanical apparatuses; and these organs themselves can be replaced temporarily or permanently by machines or transplants. Less spectacular but just as impressive are the advances in medicines and radiology.

Many of these treatments directly abet the maintenance and preservation of human life, and their extraordinary effectiveness gives rise to the whole question about a doctor's failure to use them. In a real sense, the doctor holds the patient's life in his hands.

Quite justifiably, people have begun to talk about the physician's manipulation of human life. Some critical voices have been raised, demanding that limits be set on the last-ditch measures available to physicians. If the physician were to go beyond these limits in treating the human organism, he would be guilty of overstepping his bounds. If the instances described above do not convey the force of this viewpoint, we might suggest this composite but truly possible case: Picture a man breathing by artificial means, with only half a brain, paralyzed arms, and no lower torso—but alive!

This is no sick joke; it is a real possibility that must be thought through. The question is all the more urgent because there is a second viewpoint which is defended just as vigorously. It maintains that a doctor may never overlook or bypass any procedure that can prolong the life of the patient. If he does, he is practicing euthanasia—which has met with justifiable condemnation.

A third viewpoint maintains that we cannot lay down any universally valid answer for such questions, because each individual case is different. Therefore each physician must answer to his own medical conscience for what he does. In a certain sense, this conclusion is correct, but it does not rule out the possibility of a basic, underlying conception. The individuality of each case is recognized in medicine, yet we still quite rightly look for general treatment procedures—with greater or lesser success.

Moreover, a little criticism should not tempt us to jump on the bandwagon with those who refer such decisions back to the purely personal decision of the physician, or who feel these last-ditch situations should be judged from a purely medical point of view. They are forgetting that such a standpoint already represents a basic decision for or against the unconditional prolongation of human life.

The question, then, is whether a physician should strike a blow for life or for death in a given case of this sort. A few decades ago, the question would have seemed absurd. Today it is an urgent question for the physician, and he is mistaken if he thinks he can avoid it. The prolongation of human life, as a universally valid aim of medical treatment, has now become a moot question. We must describe the task of the physician so comprehensively and convincingly that we will have a basis for judging all his medical decisions—even the extreme ones demanded of modern medicine.

The difficulty lies in our recognition of the fact that such a basis cannot be derived solely from all that the natural sciences tell us about man. Such a basis presupposes extra-medical decisions on which there is no unanimous agreement. Despite this, we must look for some position that will, at the very least, be acceptable to the largest possible number of people in our pluralistic world.

II
THE CRITERION: MAN'S WELFARE

Our first basic postulate would probably be acceptable to everyone: The goal of all medical treatment is the welfare of the human person. But this raises questions on which no ready agreement can be found. What is man's welfare: his life or his good health? Quite often a man's life can only be maintained at the expense of his good health. Some would regard a given patient's situation as worth living, others would regard it as not worth living, while a third group would challenge our right to judge that it is not worth living. We have already seen where this can lead.

The confusion becomes complete when we introduce religious considerations—e.g., the will of God. One group says that God wills every life to be preserved. A second group maintains that humble acceptance of sickness and death is a duty for Christians. And when these two differing proponents of God's will come up against a physician or patient who has no use for religion, all three are lost in bewilderment.

How are we to arrive at a solution? Revelation provides no direct statement as to how to judge these last-ditch medical procedures. Thus we must draw conclusions from the biblical portrait of man, from the basic ethical instinct of man (of Christians, in particular), and from our natural reasoning process.

The last-mentioned basis, man's natural reason, has particular significance for contemporary questions in medical ethics, since it is most likely to provide a basis of agreement between men even those who are not Christians.

How do we determine what the welfare of man is? We must deduce it from his nature. And we must start out by examining our anthropological concept of man, for it contains several different assertions: man is a biological being; man is a spiritual and personal being; man is a social being; man is an historical being. First and foremost, man is a unified being. He is a concrete unity, not a conglomeration of parts (e.g., body, mind and soul). Adopting both the viewpoint of the natural sciences and the viewpoint of the arts, we must see him as a unified whole, and we can actually experience him as such.

Only by seeing all these different aspects can we discern his authentic nature. We can observe such natural phenomena as dignity, love, freedom and biological processes, but we cannot grasp their full meaning by using the methods of natural science alone. Man's full development of his self in history, in contact with his fellow men, is not a superfluous duty; it is one of the essential tasks that makes man what he is.

This rounded anthropological view of contemporary science corresponds fully with the biblical portrait of man. Keeping in mind what we have just said, we can make use of a traditional formula: Anything and everything that is in accordance with man's "nature" is morally right and fosters man's welfare. But part of the irrelinquishable nature of man is that he is not just a biological being, and that of his very nature he has the right and the duty to master his biological nature.

Therefore we should not use the contrasting notions of "natural" and "artificial" in evaluating the ethics of medical treatment; we should rather make a distinction between "meaningful" and "meaningless" measures. Our view of man is necessarily a multi-dimensional one. In seeking an ethical standard, then, we are going contrary to man's nature if we focus exclusviely on its biological side and formulate our ethical norms on that basis alone. However much the biological aspect of man may tell us, it does not tell us everything.

In modern medicine, then, any medical procedure that serves the well-being of the *whole* man is justified, in principle at least. And this holds true even if we are talking about artificial hearts and procedures affecting heredity. The degree of intervention itself cannot provide us with ethical limits—as if it were permissible to go so far and no further. In terms of the whole man, the chances and risks, the gains and losses, of a given procedure may and must be weighed in terms of the concrete situation, so that we can decide whether it serves the welfare of the patient. To be sure, a given procedure may be prompted by an authoritarian conviction, but this is not necessarily related to the degree of interference involved.

III
"KILLING" VERSUS "ALLOWING TO DIE"

Now if, in principle, a physician is justified in using any and every measure no matter how extreme, must he not use such procedures whenever the patient's life is endangered, if the non-use of them will mean the patient's death? Wouldn't his refusal to use them amount to euthanasia and fall under the fifth commandment? Does this not limit our thesis that the welfare of man is the norm of medical treatment?

Here we cannot possibly delve into all the complicated questions that crop up, such as: Are there ethical prohibitions that are universally valid and know no exceptions? Does mercy killing, done out of pity or at the express wish of the patient, fall under such a prohibition? And, in fact, there is no need to go into these questions, for the refusal to use life-prolonging procedures certainly cannot be viewed as killing in the above sense.

Many people find it hard to see the distinction between "killing" and "allowing a person to die" (if the prolongation of life no longer serves the welfare of the human being). The correctness of this distinction is probably best brought out by showing what would happen if we equated "killing" and "allowing to die".

Christian ethics and the overwhelming majority of doctors maintain that the directly intended killing of a patient (e.g., by an overdose of drugs) is unconditionally wrong, quite independently of the concrete situation and the patient's wishes (i.e., of his life expectancy). Now if "killing" and "allowing to die" are equated, then the same holds true for the non-use of last-ditch medical measures. The unavoidable conclusion, then, is that any physician who refuses to use last-ditch measures (e.g., artificial breathing apparatus), even when the patient's situation is hopeless, is guilty of euthanasia. For even in such hopeless cases, the doctor could probably prolong the life of the patient a little longer, and the shortness of the time span does not enter the picture.

It should not be hard to see that this would be a ridiculous situation, quite apart from the fact that the last stages would involve enormous expense and that no doctor or machine could provide meaningful therapy. When the prolongation of life must involve the sacrifice of speech and all communication with the environment, or other disturbances of the same general magnitude, we might well call it nothing more than the prolongation of pain. In such circumstances, we must ask ourselves whether such measures really serve the welfare of the patient. If the answer is no, we must abandon our attempt—meaningless in the concrete situation—to postpone the patient's death. The determination of "meaningful" and "meaningless" must be based on a human view of the situation, since no other court of appeal is available to us.

The view proposed here can also handle the objection that is sometimes made from the juridical side. Some point out that there is such a thing as killing a person by neglect. This is true, of course, but neglect implies that a person does not do something he has an obligation to do. The obligation here is not absolute; it is open to question, and it depends upon the concrete situation, as the law itself concedes. No jury would condemn a physician for not using last-ditch measures in a hopeless case, where life could only be prolonged for a few minutes more. Strictly speaking, the legal code regards only "neglect in the line of duty" as punishable, but this specification is often overlooked or forgotten.

The decision not to force the prolongation of life, when this has become meaningless or when there are weighty ethical obligations on the opposing side, also has a theological aspect, for it involves our recognition of not only technical but also human limitations. It involves the acceptance of man's creaturehood and of death. Such acceptance is credible witness only if it is rendered of one's own free will, not just when the limits of technological procedure leave no alternative. By the same token, homicide or suicide does not express a ready acceptance of death; on the contrary, both betray a desire to determine for oneself the manner and the time of one's own death.

Right here we must concede something. Because of the great technical advances in medicine, there are situations where any meaningful distinction between active killing of the patient and mere refusal to prolong his life becomes quite blurred. This is most obvious in cases where a patient's breathing is being kept up by respiratory machines and where the doctor, out of lack of thought or despair over recovery, is tempted to cut off use of the breathing apparatus. A physician will be very hesitant about taking such a step, and he will do so only in exceptional cases. The important thing is to make it clear that this seemingly active intervention would actually be a decision against further therapy, that is, a decision to allow the patient to die, rather than active homicide, and thus it would not merit basic condemnation.

A second situation where the danger of committing euthanasia is often postulated is the administration of pain-killing drugs to patients with incurable diseases. Scrupulously conscientious physicians often are reluctant to use such drugs in sufficient doses because they are afraid that they might thereby contribute to a quicker death and be guilty of manipulating a man's life irresponsibly. This fear, however, is based on a misunderstanding.

There is a world of difference between administering a drug to kill someone and administering a drug to ease pain (even if the latter course will adversely affect the patient's vital forces and thus shorten his life). The former course is to be condemned outright; the latter course is part of our duty as physicians.

IV

MAN AND HIS FELLOW MEN

Who is to apply the criterion we have laid down? Who is to determine what will serve the welfare of the whole man? First and foremost, the man himself! If serving the welfare of man means helping him to exercise the greatest possible freedom in fulfilling his life, then his freedom should not be impeded by the decision as to how it can be fostered.

Insofar as it is possible, and all the more when the procedure involves a greater degree of intervention, the doctor must respect the wishes of the patient, and he must help the patient to arrive at a decision by providing him with adequate (not necessarily complete) information. The patient, of course, may leave the decision up to the doctor, trusting in his expert knowledge, but he must do this of his own free will and not be pushed into it.

To be sure, there are situations where neither the patient nor his relatives are capable of making this decision. Then the doctor alone is obliged to make the decision, but even here he takes account of the presumed desires of the patient. Even if a physician regards the manipulation of man's biological processes as quite in order, he must avoid manipulating the patient's personal decision. To manipulate the latter would certainly be "contrary to nature", for it would turn man into an object at a time when he should be a choosing subject.

It would also be against the personal nature of man to regard him as an isolated individual and to overlook his essential relationship to his fellow men. Medical procedures, particularly the kind being considered here, affect not only the patient but also his family, other people with the same disease, and society as a whole. Mutual obligations exist between them, the patient and the doctor. To realize this, we need only think about the progress of science, scientific training, and the creation and distribution of the required finances.

Now these various aspects may well be in conflict with one another. If I devote a great deal of effort to one patient, this may reduce the chances of another patient. If I experiment on one patient, this may help another patient. If I keep some physical or mental cripple alive, may I not injure the welfare of his family or of the State? All these aspects must be considered in deciding whether to step in with a medical procedure, and this holds true for those extreme situations where the direct maintenance of life is at issue.

Talk about considering the interests of others may sound obnoxious at first, but it cannot be avoided so long as the capabilities of medical aid are limited—and it hardly seems that we will ever be done with such considerations. For the present, the necessity of choosing specific patients for a particular type of new treatment has only been made more acute by recent medical advances. The supply of artificial kidneys and suitable organ transplants is hardly a match for the number of patients who could be helped by them. Thus we must decide who will be given treatment and who will be allowed to die.

This course may seem harsh, but it is ethically defensible if the situation demands it and if it is done in a responsible way. In the process of selection, a wide variety of circumstances can and must be taken into account, but the medical chances of the individual will always be the most serious consideration. Even so, decisions in individual cases will sometimes be debatable, and they may even prove to be wrong in retrospect. However, this is basically true for every medical decision, and it does not release the physician from his responsibility.

The notion that man has a relationship with his fellow men takes on particular importance when we are talking about medical procedures that are not aimed at the welfare of the person who undergoes them. As examples, we might cite human experimentation in the broadest sense and organ transplants from a donor who is still alive. Here the medical procedure involves risks and possibly unhealthy consequences for the one who submits to it. One might well hold the viewpoint that no man may be damaged for a specific purpose, or damage himself.

But here again the case is similar to the use of pain-killing drugs that also involve disadvantages to health. In many cases, other parties or interests (scientific research, medical science) are not helped *through the damage itself*. It is simply that a given medical procedure simultaneously has desirable results in one direction and undesirable risks in another direction. Since the two aspects do not relate to the same person in this case, the gain-loss ratio must be particularly favorable. If it is not, then the procedure must be bypassed, even if this means that medical progress will not proceed as quickly as one had hoped.

Another point should be made here. When people talk about the disadvantages worked on the donor or the one who submits to experimentation, they often overlook the fact that this outlook is justified only in terms of the purely biological welfare of man. Such an approach, as we noted earlier, is not correct. All these biological disadvantages must be weighed in terms of man's overall welfare.

The donor in such cases should not be viewed as a purely biological organism. He should be viewed as a human being who finds fulfillment in life by having regard for his neighbor. His course of action can actually help him to find fulfillment if it is done for love of his neighbor. One thing is necessarily presupposed here, of course, insofar as the donor is concerned: that he is given a very clear and conscientious explanation of the possible and probable risks entailed in his action, and that these risks stand in a reasonable ratio to the hoped-for benefits.

V
When Is a Man Dead?

Medical progress has also created situations where a doctor can no longer be certain whether he is dealing with a living human being or a corpse. Once upon a time, the cessation of breathing or pulse meant definite death within a few minutes. Now, however, we can substitute machines for the functioning of the heart and lungs, thus forestalling the cessation of bodily functions and the structural decay of the bodily organs. When is such a patient dead? This was a difficult question, made all the more difficult by the fact that persons newly dead were used as donors of organs.

An answer was soon formulated. A human being is dead when his brain is dead. Out of respect for the competence of the medical profession, this answer was also accepted by jurists and theologians; discussion soon focused more on the criteria for determining when the brain was dead. However, this whole problem is not solved that simply.

The above response, equating brain death with human death, assumes that the brain is so much more important than the other organs that its death means human death, even when other organs are still functioning. Now the preeminent position of the brain can hardly be called into question. Its complicated structure and its overall integrating function justify this preeminence, and it is further underlined by the inability of the ganglia to regenerate, and the impossibility of replacing the brain's function by machines (apart from its control over breathing).

The brain's preeminence becomes especially clear when we consider its evolution and degree of development within the animal kingdom. Here the decisive factor is not its difference vis-à-vis related species; it is the fact that in phylogeny it shows a degree of evolution that is unmatched by any other organ. Brain development, in fact, is the principal criterion for phylogenetic classification.

Now a person still has every right to ask whether all these features make the brain so special that we can judge human death on the basis of this one organ. Even granting that it is a special organ, a person might still object that it is merely a quantitative difference. Even the importance of the brain's contribution to consciousness and associated mental functions could be viewed as an inadequate criterion, for its contributions play a relatively modest role in what we call living.

Another consideration is brought in here to bolster this objection. Death as the opposite of life, it is said, should be defined in the same way for all living creatures. This becomes impossible if we use brain death as our criterion, for many living organisms have no brain at all, or one which does not play the major role it does in human beings.

These weighty arguments have been used by Gerlach [1] and others to challenge and reject the accepted equation: brain death = human death. They say that we can only distinguish between partial death and total death, that brain death is only one type of partial death, and that human death comes only with total death. (Total death means the cessation of all the bodily organs.) This solidly grounded concept is clear, logical, and unassailable on the grounds of natural science.

The only question is: How much does this obviously sober definition have to offer us? To what extent does it do justice to the matter in hand? What merit does it have if we choose to use it? For our question is not raised in a vacuum, but in a given concrete situation where we must act. We must decide to keep the patient alive or to bury him. And we are not indulging in superficial pragmatism here, so long as we are looking for some unified conception that will do justice to every situation.

If we are looking for a definition of human death, then we must consider the nature of man himself. Now man's nature cannot be equated or identified with purely those aspects that come under the natural sciences. Thus a definition of human

[1] J. Gerlach, "Individualtod—Partialtod—Vita Reducta," in *Münch. Med. Wschr.* 16 (1968); "Die Definition des Todes in ihrer heutigen Problematik für Medizin und Rechtslehre," in *Arztrecht* (1968).

death that derives solely from those aspects is a caricature. Some might object here that my statement is more a profession of belief than a reasoned deduction. If it is, it is a profession of belief in a multi-dimensional portrait of man, and it cannot be provided or refuted by the natural sciences as long as they stay within their self-imposed methodological limits. Moreover, it is a profession that many people will support: specifically, all those to whom human dignity, love and other such notions mean something. They live this profession of belief, whether they express it in words or not.

Now if we reevaluate the biological arguments for the preeminence of the brain with a multi-dimensional picture of man in mind, the seemingly weak criteria take on new weight and solidity. For everything that characterizes man as such—his mental and spiritual dimensions, his personal individuality and identity—are tied in with the brain. Moreover, the other seemingly reasonable criterion—that individual death must be equated with total death for all living creatures—loses its self-evident character.

In the evolutionary scale, individuality grows in importance along with the differentiation of organisms and the signficance of psychic phenomena. A human being is an individual in a more pronounced sense than is a frog or a lower organism. The concept of "individual" is analogous, and therefore the notion of "individual death" is analogous, too.

It may be all right to equate individual death with total death in the borderline case of animals who can lose 99% of their vitality and still regenerate from the remaining 1%. In these cases, we probably do better to speak of specimens than of individuals. But as we ascend the scale of animal life, this equation loses validity. Carried to its logical consequences, it would mean that a heart donor would only die upon the death of the heart recipient, even though he had been buried long ago.

By introducing considerations about man's psychic functions, we give added weight to the biological arguments in favor of the brain's preeminence. It is all the more convincing because the added weight is not based on an accumulation of separate arguments, but on one and the same argument viewed from different standpoints. Thus we have one basic argument for saying that brain death means human death. It is not a purely scientific argument, but it holds up against any criticism.

To be sure, our thesis does not provide us with a perfect and complete solution. We know that considerable portions of the brain can be damaged without resulting in a person's death. Moreover, we must be logical and assume that certain parts of the brain can outlive a human being, just as his heart can.

Which parts of the brain can outlive the person? Are we dealing here with specific parts, or is it a matter of quantity? We know very little. Medical technology has given us new and deeper insights, but they only add to our uncertainty. Now that we are able to analyze death in slow motion, what once seemed like an instantaneous event now seems like a gradual process. Thus we now are asking what death (not dying) is: a gradual process or an instantaneous event? It is doubtful that medicine will be able to give a definitive answer to this question, even as it cannot tell us about the beginning of man's life.

But even though our solution is only an approximate one, it is quite serviceable. Despite our uncertainty as to whether there is a specific moment of death, and what it is exactly, our considerations here force us to link it up with the death of the brain. There is a safety factor, an element of certainty, in our thesis: it is tied up with the death (i.e., the cessation of the structural metabolism) of the *whole* brain.

The methodological determination of brain death must do justice to this requirement, whether it is based on clinical, electrophysiological symptoms or on recording the cessation of cerebral circulation. Despite all the technological advances, medical science is still faced with many uncertainties, and they are all the more significant when the determination of death must be made quickly.

One might well object that in these circumstances a physician could not possibly justify the premature removal of a vital organ on the grounds that the time was right for a transplant. (Quite understandably, the whole question came to a head on this issue.) The refusal to remove the organ does certainly enable us to avoid making a decision about the death of the donor. But at the same time it forces us to make a critical decision regarding the would-be receiver of the transplant. It may well take away his last chance for life.

An overly long delay, for the sake of being on the safe side, would not be a satisfactory way out, for the increased certainty regarding the death of the donor would involve increased jeopardy to the success of the transplant. Even if there were a tiny spark of life left in the patient, who was clearly and irrevocably at death's door and dead for all practical purposes, the removal of an organ at that point would not be directly intended homicide; it would be permissible homicide.

This distinction may seem too subtle and even shocking. But we should realize that there is a big difference between killing someone deliberately for whatever reason and, e.g., having a fire truck run the risk of killing a careless pedestrian as it rushes to a fire to save lives. A responsible transplant operation, which carefully weighed the chances of success, would be similar to the latter case.

Moreover, we must not forget that the decision here is ultimately a human decision, even though it rests upon biological data. Such a human decision can never enjoy mathematical certitude. It can enjoy, at best, moral certitude—that is, it must involve as much certainty as we can obtain by thinking through a question as conscientiously as possible.

This view provides no easy escape for the physician. He cannot simply talk about this matter; he must act on it. Aware that an element of theoretical uncertainty remains, and knowing that it must explore the matter further, the doctor's conscience will remain awake and vigilant; it will not be lulled to sleep by the arrogant and illusory comfort of absolute certainty.

VI

TRADITION AND AGGIORNAMENTO IN MEDICAL ETHICS

Our treatment here, obviously enough, has not solved all the problems raised by the progress of modern medicine. But that is not the task of medical ethics in any case. Like any branch of ethics, it is not a recipe book providing a detailed code of behavior; nor is it a substitute for conscientious decisions in the concrete situation. Of its very nature, it abstracts from men's experiences in given situations and deduces a basic framework of ideas from them, and this framework can only serve as a general guidepost for new concrete decisions.

Ethical conduct must always be appropriately human conduct. And since human beings, of their very nature, undergo change through history, no ethical concept can be viewed as finished and definitive. New answers must be sought for new questions, and this holds true in medicine also.

On the other hand, human change in history is not devoid of continuity. Our considerations in this paper are strengthened rather than weakened by the fact that traditional elements clearly perdure in our solution. Though the overall problem may have changed drastically, we still have the principle of totality, the importance of means and ends, the principle of double effect, and the distinction between causing and allowing to happen.

To be sure, the maintenance of traditional principles is justified only if we use them correctly. We cannot pile them one atop the other unthinkingly. We must clearly show that they converge toward a single unified outlook that has particular weight in contemporary thought: the indivisible wholeness of concrete human beings, the unity imposed upon human conduct by man's intention, and the consequent significance of this intention for every ethical judgment.

Willem Ariëns/*Vught, Netherlands*

The Function of the Judge in Our Time

Anyone embarking upon an examination of the demands that contemporary society places on the law is bound to proceed on the premise that the workings of the judiciary must continue to provide what has been traditionally expected from it: The dispensation of justice with complete impartialty and with a conscientious application of the existing legal guidelines.

I

THE JUDGE AND THE SENSE OF JUSTICE

These legal guidelines need to be embodied in laws. Such laws will have to be applied according to objectives which can be deduced from the drafting of their provisions and the history of their origins. Where this gives rise to injustice, this must be blamed on the legislator, since it is not in the power of the court to give a ruling which, however unjust, conflicts with the law.

There are few cases where the law is so clear that the decision in a particular dispute can be given without further ado; at such times, legal provisions will then have to be interpreted in a manner which while consistent with their general objective, would nevertheless appear to fit precisely the case in question.

It is therefore timely to reflect that provisions of statute law have to serve not only for the times that gave birth to them, but also for later ages in which changed circumstances may have given rise to changed concepts of law, and that these provisions can consequently be interpreted with a degree of flexibility which will allow their application in a manner consistent with what has then come to be regarded as just.

That which has come to be regarded as just may gradually become such a feature of social behavior that one can virtually describe it as a rule of conduct which society requires to be observed. This makes up the common law which supplements statute law and, along with it, governs the administration of justice.

When neither statute law nor the common law is of any avail in providing a direct answer to a dispute, then the judge is himself obliged to "find" the right legal ruling and, in the process, render a judgment which, while fitting into the general framework of defined law or precedent gives expression to the "ius in causa positum".

Common law and adjudicated cases create an unmistakable bond with respect and understanding of the law by the people. Between justice on the one hand, and respect and understanding of the law on the other, there is an indissoluble link.

When this sense of justice changes during the course of time in the light of changing concepts of right and wrong, then the question about the function of the judge in our time demands not only from the legislator but also from the judge the keenest possible understanding of that particular time and, so far as the law will permit it, the rendering of judgments that are in the spirit of the age. Only in this way will the judge be acting in a manner that is acceptable to his contemporaries and likely to engender confidence in the judiciary. Both of these factors are matters of prime necessity if a healthy respect for the law is to be maintained. For, where this is lacking, the tendency to take the law into one's own hands, even if only in civil disputes, rather than turn to others for a ruling, will gain the upper hand. In this way a feeling of legal insecurity will give rise to a rapid spread of anxiety.

In our own time particularly, this eternally important question of confidence in the law has been going through an obvious period of evolution. In former times, and still today in some more or less primitive societies, that confidence was and remains anchored in the formal authority with which the judge was armed by virtue of his office: when the judge had spoken, justice had been done. In more advanced societies the opinions of a number of select social groups—such as educators, lawyers and the like— have subjected the decisions reached by the judiciary to expert criticism. Moreover, as people generally come to acquire greater confidence in themselves and a higher degree of education, the influence they exercise on the evolution of a general sense of justice increases and their involvement with the motivation of legal decisions becomes more direct.

A factor of particular significance in our own day is the critical attitude which society as a whole has come to adopt toward any exercise of authority, including the law; such an attitude springs, if I am not mistaken, from a basic lack of confidence in formal authority. This is due either to the fact that the standards to which those in power refer when wielding their authority are no longer regarded as generally acceptable, or because people, in a prevailing revolutionary atmosphere, are not prepared to submit themselves to traditional legal norms until their merits have once again been carefully scrutinized and found acceptable. This is why ordinary people are seeking a degree of participation in many aspects of life—for example, in the political and commercial fields—including many where the opportunity to do so does not yet exist.

As far as the law is concerned, this form of participation exists in many countries in the shape of various forms of a jury system. In the Netherlands, where this system is not practiced, several voices have recently called for its introduction. Much more widespread has been the call for more information to enable people to decide for themselves, more clearly than ever before, whether the decisions of the judiciary can be accepted with confidence. In this way, it would no longer be the office of the judge as such but, at least to a certain extent, the intrinsic value of the work of the judge which would come to form the new yardstick.

Clearly, it is impossible to treat all legal judgments in the same way. For example, it is easier for laymen to express valid opinions on criminal law than on matters of civil law, since in the latter case it is primarily the interests of the parties to the dispute that are involved, and civil law has, furthermore, a strong technical and juridical character. Moreover, it is, in criminal law that the most essential interests of society are involved, and it is as much the suitability of the punishment for a particular offense as the question of proving its commission that is of direct concern to the community as a whole. Men have always been fascinated by criminal law and drawn by the desire to witness its application by means of public hearings.

It is now time to consider more closely what conditions the judiciary must seek to satisfy if its members wish to preserve the indispensable trust of the great mass of the people today.

In view of the differences in nature and in function which we noted above between criminal law and the rest of the law, it seems desirable to investigate separately the requirements for each of these two branches of the judiciary.

II

CRIMINAL LAW

As we have already seen, it is of the greatest importance for crime to be punished. A first prerequisite to this end is objective proof that a crime has really been committed. From this it follows that in many legal systems a simple admission of guilt by the accused is not regarded as sufficient evidence for his conviction; supporting evidence is required to prove with reasonable certitude that his confession is based upon real facts.

Furthermore, the handling of a criminal case is protected with numerous safeguards, designed to ensure that the rights of the accused in his defense are fully respected. Finally, the public hearing of these cases guarantees that both the public and the press have the possibility of exercising some measure of control over the observance of the law and the just treatment of the accused.

The importance of this last factor cannot be sufficiently emphasized. The law's formal requirements may be observed with the utmost scrupulousness, but when this is not coupled with a dignified and above all humane attitude toward the man who is the subject of prosecution at the trial, then the law, as it reveals itself in the open court, will have fallen below the level that men have come—today more than ever—to expect from it. To question the accused calmly and without disparagement, without the prosecution seeking to force the impression that he "has really done it", and to allow the accused every opportunity to defend himself and, in the process, to take him "seriously" even when one has real doubts about his honesty—these, more than anything else, will engender public confidence in the judge's impartiality and freedom from preconceived ideas and, as a result, confidence in him as a man who, whatever his final decision, has nonetheless afforded the accused every opportunity to justify himself.

And so we come now to the final verdict. The law requires that it should be adequately motivated and that it should be pronounced in public; it further requires not only an analysis of the proof of guilt, together with precise indications of the nature of the evidence that has been submitted, but also a reasoned explanation of the type of penalty or measure imposed by way of punishment.

It is of course impossible to expect that the mere reading of the judge's verdict will give the accused—or the public—sufficient insight into the merits of his reasoning or the appropriateness of his sentence. This will apply more than ever when—as it is indeed difficult to avoid in the majority of criminal cases—the judge's ruling is limited to one or more routine legal provisions; in them the guilt of the accused and the appropriate nature of the sentence that has been pronounced may be set out in a way that offers no further insight into the case. This makes it all the more important that the judge, after he has delivered his verdict, should explain in "layman's" language what the case has really been all about, and why his particular ruling, and no other, is, in his view, the right one for the case that has just been heard in his court.

Finally, a word must be said about the sentence or measures to be applied. This would normally, by its very nature, be little noticed by the public at the time of judgment, except in those cases where it appears far too heavy or too light. But that to which public attention certainly is directed is whether in broadly parallel cases similar sentences (or measures) are applied. This springs from a fully understandable desire which corresponds to a basic notion of justice expressed in the phrase "suum cuique tribuere". Stated in the vernacular, this roughly means: "What is sauce for the goose is sauce for the gander".

The exceptional importance of this need to have a fair system of justice is currently very much in evidence in the hearing of traffic offenses, particularly in cases where drivers have driven vehicles after such excessive consumption of alcohol that they are no longer able to properly control them: in short, "drunken driving". A motorist found driving in such a state may, in addition to the temporary withdrawal of his driving license, be given an unconditional sentence of imprisonment by Judge A. If, however, he is able to escape beyond the latter's area of jurisdiction and is not caught until reaching an adjacent area under the jurisdiction of Judge B, then a very different decision— such as, for instance, his conditional release subject perhaps to the payment of a fine—is not excluded, and may even be quite probable if Judge B, in contrast with Judge A, considers that such a conditional sentence, perhaps holding out a real threat for such drivers for a period of several years should they be caught again, constitutes the best means to prevent repetition of the offense. Where two such different sentences are meted out to two motorists caught in identical circumstances, then nothing is left of the theory that what is "sauce for the goose is sauce for the gander"; in the process a judicial injustice has clearly occurred, and public opinion is immediately aroused.

To find a solution to this serious problem, which arises from a particular judge's freedom to define the degree of criminality involved, is not a simple matter. It is possible for the legislator to restrict the judge's discretion by laying down pre-determined penalties that allow little flexibility. However, this solution could well turn out to be worse than the evil that existed before, since the cure would then have been effected by means of a serious rigidifying of the law, leaving little or no room for flexibility in shading the severity of sentences, as might be called for by particular circumstances.

In Holland, where the freedom of the judge is regarded as a matter of the highest importance, a solution to this problem is being sought through personal consultations among the judicial authorities concerned with criminal matters. Designed to attempt to reach a certain broad similarity of sentencing policy, their point of departure is that for a given offense there should be a specific sentence or fine; however, these penalties may be modified in the light of special mitigating circumstances.

Only time will show whether this method of approach will provide a satisfactory solution. It is evident, however, that a solution will have to be found soon, since the existing legal injustices are manifest for all to see and are seriously undermining the authority of the law.

A movement in this direction would leave less room than before for shading the severity of sentences. Circumstances may nonetheless make such a development necessary, since the rapid growth in vehicular traffic—and the enormous increase in traffic offenses that seems to be so inextricably linked to it—are generating ever stronger pressures to find a form of legal sanction that is better equipped to deal with this new situation than that provided by the cautiously serene atmosphere of the courtroom. Apart from the cases of "drunken driving" which we have just discussed—and which, in view of the serious consequences they may have for the driver and his victims, cannot be dealt with outside the courts—there may, and in my opinion will be, many cases where traffic offenses can be dealt with without the need for intervention by the courts.

Such offenses, for example, could be dealt with by the police, provided that the provisions of the law were strictly complied with. This would result in a somewhat inflexible system—elementary, if you like—and yet not unacceptable, if only because there is no other solution in sight. The time has passed when we can leave the ordinary courts laden with extensive and burdensome activities which are unworthy of their professional attention. Their essential task lies in the assessment of evidence and proven facts, in the weighing of conflicting interests, and in the making of decisions as to the degree of discretion that may be exercised *in concreto*. This is a far cry from dealing with simple offenses which not only could but should be easily and quickly settled. And without falling into the opposite extreme of a system of computers, we should not be afraid to release the courts from such matters, provided that the element of human intervention is retained.

We stated earlier that normally the severity of the sentence or measure decreed by a judge remains outside the scrutiny of public opinion. This is not entirely true. Public opinion, in this context, is shaped not least by a legal intelligentsia consisting in the first instance of a group of experts in criminal law and criminology. It is this group in particular which has argued, especially since the end of World War II, in favor of some relaxation in the provisions of the criminal law and has emphasized in so doing the supreme importance of rehabilitating the individuals concerned so as to prevent them relapsing into crime; hence the desirability of making greater use of conditional or suspended sentences, to which can be linked certain specified conditions of social conduct and subjection to supervision during the period of rehabilitation.

Without a doubt, it is to the effects of this trend on the sciences of criminal law and criminology that we can attribute, at least in Holland, the widespread substitution of conditional for unconditional sentences; the results to date encourage the hope that further progress will be made in this direction.

III
Civil Law

In contrast with criminal law, it has been traditionally accepted that in civil law cases all parties should be required to be *domini litis*. In these cases the issue is not whether the interest of the community demands that action should be taken to punish a transgression against the law, but rather whether a particular private interest can claim the protection of the law. It is up to a plaintiff to say whether and to what extent he will invoke the protection of the law, and it is up to a defendant to decide whether he will, there and then, accept the plaintiff's claim or fight it either wholly or in part. If the facts as they are alleged are admitted by both parties, then they are also accepted by the judge, provided that they are "formally" correct; in such cases there is then no need to establish their objective proof. In cases where the issues in dispute do need to be proved, the onus of proof—and the risk this involves—lies squarely on the party that brought the case before the court; however, the same party is free to decide how it will set about obtaining such proof.

Until recently, the generally accepted assumption was that the issue for decision was not so much the truth of the facts of the case but rather what the two parties to the dispute regarded as the real issue. This had a number of consequences: the plaintiff was bound, in principle, by whatever he had stated and claimed in his original pleadings; no upward revision of his claim or modification to the basis of his case could be entertained. The defendant was similarly bound, in principle, to his opening position. And to make matters worse, all this was accompanied by conditions which, if they were not scrupulously observed, could lead to the case being brought abruptly to a close without any pronouncement by the judge upon the issue at stake.

Against this procedural background the judge had a role that was essentially passive: his task was simply to apply the law to accepted facts or to facts that had in fact been proved by the parties to the dispute by their own methods.

For many years now a gradual change has been taking place. It has come to be regarded as increasingly unsatisfactory that the judge should be expected a give a ruling about a case when it was far from certain that the matter put to him was in fact what was really in dispute between the parties concerned, or that it accurately reflected the issue at stake; no less undesirable was the idea that the judge should not be permitted to intervene when he came across gaps in the evidence submitted by one of the parties, or when he formed the clear impression that the matter could be amicably settled, even though the parties to the dispute showed no signs of being prepared to stop their expensive and fruitless feud, especially in cases based on a particular situation that was no longer applicable.

These and other similar objections led gradually to a more or less radical restriction, at least in continental legal systems, of the passive role of the judge. He became authorized to intervene in cases of unreasonable procedural delays and to oblige parties to appear in person either to have them give evidence or to attempt to bring them to an amicable compromise. Greater use was also made of the judge's power to call for evidence, either from witnesses whose appearance he considered desirable, or from documents he wished to consult.

At the same time, upward revisions of claims and modifications to the positions adopted at the beginning of the hearing of a case also became permissible. A further sign of the growing opposition to legal formalism was the fact that the rejection or final dismissal of a plaintiff's case as a result of his failure to observe certain formal legal provisions became steadily less frequent, except in those cases where their observation was essential to safeguard a specific interest of the other party to the dispute. The trend illustrated by this reversal in attitudes was clearly intended to give greater legal power to the social aspects of communal law.

Legal differences can be likened to so many knots in the network of communal life; they must be untangled as quickly as possible, and it is to this process of unraveling that the law must at all times be directed. The fact that the parties to a dispute are not *obliged* to submit their differences to the judge does not mean that, once the case has come before the court, they can determine its further course in every respect; however, the idea that the judge should have the power to intervene actively in the case, at least up to a certain point, is no longer disputed.

IV

New Claims on the Work of the Judiciary?

After this necessarily rather detailed introduction, we are continually confronted with the related question of whether our modern age, within the framework of overall judicial activity, has also developed new claims on the work of the judiciary in civil disputes. It seems to me that this question must be answered emphatically in the affirmative.

First of all, neither the law's customary inertia nor the often superfluous detail of much written and oral evidence submitted by legal advisers is reconcilable with the tempo of modern life. In view of the comparatively few important or complicated matters whose preparation and hearing inevitably require a great deal of time, it could, and indeed must, be possible to shorten legal procedure in the vast majority of cases, preferably by shortening the time allowed for parties to the dispute to conclude or submit their evidence, by reducing rigid adherence to formal legal provisions to a strict minimum, and, finally, by obliging the parties to the dispute to be at hand during the hearing of the case on all occasions in the hope that their presence might facilitate a settlement.

These points require, above all, a great degree of flexibility in legal procedure. This involves maximum delays for reaching a settlement, provided that these can be varied when circumstances appear to warrant it, liberty for the parties to the dispute to select the points at issue which they wish to lay before the judge, but liberty also for the judge to take any steps which he considers to be of importance in enabling him to render a fair decision. Furthermore, if the objective of a more rapid and flexible judicial procedure is to be achieved, it will be necessary to replace the system of a panel of three judges, which is still widely used, by one with a single presiding judge.

A lawsuit conducted along these lines could make immediate and close consultation between the judge and the parties to the dispute and their legal advisers an essential prerequisite. The judge would then cease to be like an umpire in a tennis match, sitting inviolate in his high chair, watching the game and only giving his decision at the end of the game. He would become instead an organ of authority involved in the contest from the very beginning, armed not only with the power but also with the authority to guarantee the fair conduct of the case and, where necessary, to intervene, but doing so—in view of the private interests involved—in close consultation with the parties concerned. No further examples are necessary to show that a single judge—so much more readily accessible to either counsel should they wish to consult him, and so much better poised for immediate intervention—is much more fitted than a panel of judges to achieve this end.

We are a long way from the situation in which the development of civil law along the lines we have just indicated will receive general approbation; imminent realization of this situation is nowhere in sight. However, there are signs that justify some optimism about the possible breakthrough of these modern concepts. Thus, the 1963 Congress of the Union Internationale des Magistrats came, *inter alia,* to the conclusion that the civil law should be "rapide et efficace" in its operation, that formal legal provisions should be allowed to delay court procedure as little as possible, and that legal decisions could, in certain specified fields, be entrusted to a single judge.

V

CONCLUSION

We have seen that the task of the judge in our time does not differ in its essentials from that which has traditionally been regarded as his responsibility: impartially to render everyone his due, while observing the laws which the people have accepted as necessary to maintain order in society.

The rule of law draws its essential significance from the way in which it is applied *in concreto*. It is for this reason that each and every decision of the judge acts like a touchstone of the "just merit" of the law invoked. It is also possible that, weighed against the provisions of the law, the judge's decision will be found to have been too lenient. The people's confidence in their judges is therefore a factor that must be considered in every case.

While in less developed societies this confidence is anchored in the formal authority of the judge by virtue of his position, elsewhere it has become dependent on the intrinsic merit of judicial decisions, judged by men competent to do so, as well as by others who imagine themselves thus qualified. It follows that the vital need for men now, in a time characterized by a refusal to recognize authority, to have—and to have good reason to have—confidence in the administration of justice is more clearly illustrated than ever before.

We have examined the new requirements with which the law has been confronted as a result of these developments under the separate heads of criminal and civil law. In the case of criminal law, the manner in which the examination of witnesses called before the court is conducted is of exceptional importance: strict observance of the prescribed provisions of the law, tempered with a humane attitude toward the accused in keeping with the dignity of the law, and, finally, when it comes to the sentence, however appropriate it may be, the inclusion of a verbal explanation that will help to make it clearer and more readily acceptable.

In the second place, there must be similar penalties in similar cases, regardless of whether or not the cases come up before different judges. The judge's freedom to exercise discretion in criminal cases must, in the interests of justice and fairness, be subjected to certain limits.

In the third place, the frightening increase in offenses makes it essential that the courts should be relieved of the task of dealing with them; given the relatively simple nature of this type of work, such offenses could easily be left to the police to handle.

Finally, the punishment of crime with an eye to the rehabilitation of the criminal, including the device of conditional sentences, is completely in line with contemporary developments in the field of criminal law.

In the domain of civil law, we have hopes of eventually seeing a situation of a judge seeking to find a solution to the real dispute that has arisen between the parties concerned as quickly as possible, acting in close consultation both with them and with their legal advisers, and much more ready to put formal difficulties to one side than is presently the case.

Every legislator will have to judge for his own legal community whether and to what extent further provisions are required to provide the necessary legal basis for the desiderata which we have set out in this article. But the crucial issue, as much in the field of criminal law as in that of civil law, will be the attitude of the judge in his approach to the implementation of such law. He must be conscious of the fact that not only his decision *in concreto,* but also the manner in which it has been reached, must be in accord with the sense of justice of the community of which he is himself a part.

José-María Solozábal/*Bilbao, Spain*

Public Service

The fact that man is an eminently social being has always led him to form associations of one sort or another, for a variety of purposes, to enable him to satisfy his needs more fully and reach a degree of attainment impossible to the individual acting on his own. Political society—that is, the State—has, in one form or another, always been one of the essential modes of social organization, indeed an elemental and basic one in itself, while complementing other forms of human association.

This means that a considerable and fundamental part of the ends that man has to pursue in society has to be pursued on the political level. Or, to put it another way, a very important part, both qualitatively and quantitatively, of the common good, or good obtained through communal means, has to be pursued within political society, and has to be the specific aim of this society. This has always been the case, and so there has always been an essential link between the common good and the State, the principal agent of this common good. This fact is, in principle, independent of any particular form of political and social organization.

The degree of aims to be achieved through politics, however, can vary, which means that the extent of State intervention in the social and economic life of the country has not always been constant. The crisis of the liberal concept of society and the State is a fact; this has brought about the rise of political and socioeconomic structures in which the State reserves to itself ends and aims which had previously fallen into the ambit of private activity. There is no need to point to countries with rigidly centralizing regimes to see the truth of this: even in countries whose declared allegiance is to the cult of personal freedom, public intervention is on the increase in social and economic processes, with varying degrees of coercion involved.

Pope John XXIII pointed to the growing socialization of the world and the ever increasing density of the texture of social relations in *Mater et Magistra*. This statement can be qualified, and to a certain extent completed, by saying that our societies are also becoming increasingly political. This brings with it a constant enriching, in depth and extension, of the common good—hence the forthright declaration in the *Constitution on the Church in the Modern World* that no one can now be content with a "merely individualistic morality". The social virtues have an ever increasing importance in regulating human relationships in the bosom of a society that has an increasing number of increasingly important functions to carry out.

In order to carry out its aims, the State needs the cooperation of particular individuals to be its executive arm, and these are known as public servants. I am not concerned here with those servants of the State whose mission is specifically political, and who work in government rather than in administration. But just as political society sets itself a wide range of aims, some of which belong to organizations properly part of the State, while others belong to infra- or para-State bodies, so the concept of public service has to be wide enough to take in those serving in these other organizations.

I am not seeking here to give a juridical definition of the idea of public service, but to deal wtih the moral aspects of the behavior of those who serve public bodies, whose function is thereby closely linked to the attainment of the common good.

The widening of the functions of the State has undoubtedly brought with it a widening of the moral question of public behavior, including the behavior of individuals in their relations with administrative bodies. This means that the morality of the behavior of public servants has also acquired new aspects and shades of application. This follows from the fact that the pursuit of the common good depends more and more on the actions of the State and its ancillaries.

Until the latter part of the 18th century, public servants were few in number, both because the State carried out relatively limited functions, and because certain social classes and individuals performed tasks that can be called public without receiving any payment from the State—the aristocracy, the military and the clergy. This state of affairs changed with the French Revolution, partly due to the fact that these classes had lost their influence, and partly because the number and complexity of public functions grew, requiring more and more people with more specialized training.

In modern States, public servants have an enormous responsibility for the good ordering of society, both because they themselves form a large social class and because the number of services that depend on them is enormous and involves an enormous quantity of money, either under the direct administration of the State, or administered by its various ancillary bodies. Today we insist—and rightly so—on the social aspect or function of the professions, just as one talks of the social role of property. But what can be important in the other professions without being role-defining is just this in the case of the public servant: his professional ethic is defined by his function, which is primordially and essentially social. Some part or aspect of the common good depends on the right behavior of any professional body, but not with the same degree of dependence as on the behavior of public servants. This is one of the prime reasons for his moral responsibility; the other resides in his contract of service—explicit or implicit—with the administrative body he works for.

A study of the moral responsibility of the public servant will naturally tend to concentrate on the virtue of justice, as this is obviously of primary importance in his case, though far from exhausting the field of natural morality, let alone of Christian perfection. I propose to utilize the categories of justice that might be called traditional, even though I believe that a restatement of the concept and classes of justice is a necessity for our time, however difficult it might be.

I

The Public Servant and the State

The root of the public servant's responsibility to the State is his contract of service (or whatever form of agreement is current), which is binding on both parties. The public servant undertakes to carry out a particular mission in the direct and immediate service of the State, looking after its interests in a particular field, and in the indirect and mediate service of the common good, this being the *raison d'être* of the State. In exchange for this he receives the right to fair remuneration, and perhaps to various privileges as well. In these relationships the virtue of fidelity comes into play, but so does commutative justice. The public servant can be an unjust source of damage vis-à-vis the State, both by omission and commission. I am not going to linger here on the well-known duties of the public servant in the carrying out of his duties, questions of professional formation and dedication, problems of administrative corruption, and so on, all of which would give full rein to tendentious casuistry. I would rather examine certain specific questions, some rather delicate ones, all closely tied to beneficial development of social life.

The efficiency and moral integrity of public servants in carrying out their duties comes from three factors (besides, of course, their own consciences): the procedure by which they are selected, the rewards they receive for their services, and the degree of control to which they are subject.

The selection or appointment methods by which public servants come to occupy their posts are of particular importance. As the results will affect the common good, it is clear that the whole of society has an interest in the methods adopted, but so have those who might be considered eligible. One has to make a distinction between the legal procedures laid down and the application of these procedures. The first concerns the drawing up of legal norms, while the second concerns the process of applying them, which will concern another set of public servants whose function it is to see that legal provisions are complied with. Whether candidates are chosen on the basis of examination results, interviews or any other procedure, it is obvious that the general interest will best be protected by the freedom of these procedures from any kind of outside interest or pressure.

Linked to this question is that of whether public service should be for a limited period of time or permanent, and whether it should be seen as a political or a technical function. I should say that the more positions that are depoliticized—that is to say, not tied to the regime or political party in power—the better the common good is served. This means that more positions will be permanent in character, which they could not be if they were tied to the fortunes of a political party, although it may be that it is considered prudent to set a limit to the period covered by the contract of engagement.

If public servants receive inadequate financial reward, the way is opened to administrative corruption, of which there is serious danger in our highly bureaucratized societies. Even if the public servant enjoys certain advantages compared to his counterpart in private business, such as security of employment or honors, it still seems to me that his financial reward should be not less than his qualifications would earn him in the private sector. He is entitled to this on account of the responsibility he bears for the common good; moreover, this alone entitles the State to make demands on him in the way of dedication, application and care in his work.

One way of ensuring that public servants approach their work in the correct way is, of course, to ensure that they are efficiently overseen. This form of control should perhaps take different forms. First, there is control from within the organization itself, through unions or professional bodies which draw up professional codes of behavior and set up their own commissions or courts of inquiry to ensure that their standards are adhered to. Public servants themselves are naturally the people most concerned in keeping the standards of their profession as high as possible. This control can be complemented by control from outside in the form of honest criticism in the communications media of the country. The mere possibility of criticism can be an effective guarantee of right behavior, particularly in the higher echelons of public service.

The public servant is often in a position where his work brings him knowledge of facts, decisions, etc., whose disclosure, even to one other person, could damage the State or certain individuals. This means that he must take the code of professional secrecy seriously. Not only must he not divulge such information, but he must not take advantage of his privileged position to use the information for personal gain, particularly if others will suffer through his doing so.

One question that can pose delicate problems is that of the public servant's relationship to the regime or political party in power. It must be remembered that the public servant owes loyalty and fidelity to the State, and to the common good through the State. But at any given moment the administrator of the common good is the government of the day. It will not always be easy to determine where activities of the government as the administrative authority of the common good end and its activities as a particular regime or party in power begin. But if there is a case of clear-cut opposition between these two sets of activities, then the public servant must always bear in mind that his service is to the common good and its attendant values rather than to party political advantage, even if he happens to share the political convictions of that party.

It seems to me that the most difficult situation in which a public servant can become involved is when he is forced to apply unjust laws, or, in the extreme case, to serve an oppressive regime. In general moral terms, no citizen can be obliged to comply with a law that is manifestly unjust (except in the exceptional circumstance where his disobedience would lead to an even greater evil), but it is not considered immoral for him to submit to that law, unless his submission brings about something essentially wrong in itself and harms someone else (the citizen again, when all is said and done), and unless an attitude of general passive resistance would be effective in bringing about a more just situation. But the public servant is in a different situation: in the first place, he is not the person who has to comply with the law, but one who has to make the ordinary citizen comply with it; in the second, his relationship with the State is of a special character lacking to that of the private citizen. A third aspect that might be borne in mind is that the resistance of public servants *en masse* is likely to be more effective than the resistance of the ordinary citizens who have to obey the law.

Unjust laws can present the public servant with an acute dilemma of conscience, and, furthermore, with the possibility of having to choose a third way other than either implementing the law or refusing to do so and thus uniting himself with the opposition to it: abandoning his post as an executive in the service of a State which is making him an instrument of oppression. If he has to arrive at a decision, he will have to consider the following criteria: an assessment of the evil that the unjust laws will entail (or the unjust regime imply), the damage that he would suffer by rebelling or abandoning his post as a State servant, and the real possibilities of forcing an improvement in the laws or in the political structure of the country itself.

There is one consideration that applies equally to public servants and to private citizens, and that is that social situations—i.e., situations affecting everyone—arise as a result of a convergence and multiplication of individual positions, and the only real way to tackle a social situation that is morally unacceptable is to attack each individual position. Social responsibilities do not exist independently of individual responsibilities, even if it is true that individual responsibility can appear to fade into the background in the overall complex of social phenomena.

In view of the numerical strength of public servants these days, one temptation to which they might be exposed would be to constitute themselves into a pressure group in support of aims or interests which are not really in their field. This danger grows with the amount of collective influence they are able to bring to bear. The armed forces of a country would represent the extreme case, and their officers can be classed as public servants. They should not form themselves into pressure groups in support of unjustified aims, nor should they put themselves at the service of other groups whose aims do not coincide with those of the State in its role of administrator of the common good.

II

THE PUBLIC SERVANT AND THE INDIVIDUAL

Relationships between public servants and individual citizens can include situations involving a solution on lines determined by the moral responsibilities of one or the other. The public servant is the instrument of the State in his dealings with the individual. These dealings will normally be regulated by legal or distributive justice, and sometimes also by commutative justice. The public servant can sometimes be responsible for trampling on a right of the individual determined by some general aspect of justice, if for instance he lets himself be guided by mixed motives or unjustified preferences in his handling of some administrative concession, if he asks for payment for something he is supposed to give away, and so on. By revealing an administrative secret, he can damage someone by placing him in a position of disadvantage through being ignorant of the secret vis-à vis the man to whom the secret has been confided. These instances are clearly ones in which—besides the general course of social justice, which looks after the interests of the common good, being per-verted—there is also the particular aspect of an individual citizen unjustly deprived of his rights.

On the other hand, the individual can also be the moral offender in his dealings with officialdom by cooperating in its unjust activities. This is a point that often affects the morality of social relationships; its importance will depend on the degree of intervention by the public servants and the general degree of administrative and general social corruption in existence at the time—for example, if an individual tries to evade a tax law by buying the cooperation—whether active or merely passive—of the official whose duty it is to secure the enforcement of this law. The individual may honestly believe that it is not a duty binding in conscience to comply with this law, since it is merely a penal law—given that one admits the existence of such a class of laws—but his action is still morally reprehensible, because the official is bound by contract to enforce observance of the law. Therefore, if the State suffered from the non-observance of the law, the official would be guilty of inflicting an injury on the State, and the individual concerned would be a real partner in this crime, with all the consequences in the way of reparation due to the injured party that this implies.

I think it is a pastorally important point that pastors should impress on their people that, whatever attitude is taken to the moral duty of observing the civil laws, it is always gravely wrong to attempt to evade civil responsibilities by corrupting an official in charge of administering them, since while the official's respon-sibility is clear, that of any accomplice is equally clear.

Another genuinely moral problem in this area is very human, difficult to overcome, and capable of invading ecclesiastical structures themselves, even though found at all levels of orga-nized society. This is the pressure that recommendations from any source can bring to bear on anyone in a position of power or authority—and public servants are in this position. It will often happen that individuals go to them to obtain advantages for themselves that could otherwise go to their competitors. Those in authority just have to learn to resist all outside blandishments and base their judgments on the fairest and most objective criteria possible. This will in many cases require a considerable degree of courage which will have to be regarded as part of their professional ethic.

It is perhaps worth mentioning a class of people who are not public servants strictly speaking, but who are not purely private individuals either, and whose activities have a considerable repercussion on the common good. These are the people who act as middlemen in a whole series of transactions: attorneys, accountants, agents, brokers, etc. A large part of all business and legal transactions have to pass through their hands; their evidence is accepted in court on the basis of their profession, and their place in society and business is established by law. The working of society obviously depends in many respects on their good behavior in the discharge of their professional functions; their failures in this respect are an offense against the common good, and therefore against social justice, although the damage they do to the State itself cannot really be equated with that which can done by a public servant properly so called. For example, a tax fraud involving a revenue official will always be a question of commutative justice, since it is this official's specific, contractual obligation to look after the interests of the Treasury, whereas a fraud perpetrated through irregularity in the conduct of an accountant or a broker would have to be considered as an offense against social justice, since these people do not work for the particular interests of the Treasury, nor are they paid by the State. Such behavior on their part would nevertheless always be immoral and even an offense against justice.

I should like to close with a particular observation on what might be called the mystique or spirit of public service. The public servant holds a unique place in society, holding a portion of the sovereignty of the State in his hands, usually permanently. If we accept the fact that the State, like any other organization, does not exist for itself, but for the individuals who compose it, then those who execute its policies must orientate their work in this same direction. The evangelical ideal of service to one's neighbor, of being useful to those with whom we come in contact, has to be a continual preoccupation of every Christian, but it has to take on a very special aspect and intensity in the public servant, being for him not only a general Christian duty, but a specific professional duty. Commutative justice will determine some of his obligations, while others will depend upon social justice and the interests of the common good, but all of his dealings with individuals must be basically guided by charity, even in those exercises of his office in which he is obliged to be coercive rather than permissive.

Wilhelm Korff/*Bonn, West Germany*

Honor Gives Way to Prestige

In the early part of the 19th century, Alexis de Tocqueville noted that "in a democratic nation there could be no *a priori* agreement on what a man's honor permits or forbids". This keen observer of the contemporary political and social world focused on "equality of social conditions" as the creative principle of modern democracy; he saw, with astonishing clarity, the casual connection between the "relative impotence of honor in democracies" and the universal mobility that characterized societies where open-ended opportunity existed.

Clear-cut and fixed standards of honor could not easily be set up in a democracy "where the citizens are constantly on the move and shifting around". The absence of a uniform public opinion and the multiplicity of opposing social and class viewpoints in a democracy necessarily lead to the displacement of honor as a central category of social ethics.

Honor

The displacement of honor as a socially oriented category in modern life is intensified all the more as man's societal progress moves out beyond the traditional class categories and frameworks. It also is related to the modern tendency, clearly evident in Fichte and the German idealist philosophers, to identify honor with the autonomy of the ego, the pathos of self-consciousness,

117

and the purely interior subjectivity of personal conscience—in short, with the tendency to focus on honor as a purely personal and interior evaluation rather than as a socially toned concept. The words of Bismarck, in his speech of November 28, 1881, exemplify the new outlook: "My honor does not rest in anyone's hands buy my own. No one can add to it or detract from it. The judgment of my own heart is all I need."

Now whatever we may think about the validity and ethical nature of this attitude, we cannot overlook the fact that it strips the concept "honor" of its traditional function. Originally it was meant to express a social estimation of the individual and his life in public. If we go back to the classical tradition in ethics, we find that honor was not primarily virtue or a personal conviction; it was primarily an "external good" (Aristotle, Thomas Aquinas) upon which the social life of a man depended, and it varied from individual to individual within a given cultural framework.

From this primary meaning there flowed certain internal attitudes that corresponded with the external good: magnanimity, dignity, uprightness, honorableness, ethical pride, self-respect and "internal honor". These internal attitudes regulated and controlled the morality of men's claims to honor in the course of history. Despite all the variations and fluctuations of history, honor retained the same basic structure. It could well be defined as follows: *Honor is the estimation of a man, formed and evidenced by other men on the basis of his merits. It is manifested objectively in his social status, and subjectively in his personal estimation of his own worth.*

Prestige

Despite the evolution of a pluralistic world and its varied standards of social evaluation, the basic structure of this concept of honor is still maintained in the contemporary notion of prestige. This is evident in the fact that prestige is often identified with social recognition and esteem. In short, prestige has taken over many of the connotations that were once attached to honor as an "external good". Nonetheless, prestige is a term with its own specific connotations, and they can only be understood adequately against the background of a changed social order and man's self-estimation within it.

The word "prestige" is French, and it originally meant "deception", "illustion" and even "magic". It ultimately derives from the Latin word *prestigiae* which denoted "feats of wonder" and the "conjuring tricks" of jugglers and entertainers. These somewhat negative overtones still cling to the word, insofar as it is used to signify forms of social recognition that lack any ultimate moral legitimation—e.g., buying lavish goods because they are prestige symbols, or trying to work one's way up in the social register.

For a long time, however, prestige has meant something more than these superficial social evaluations. It has become a general designation of the social evaluation and social status of a man, as determined by the people around him. In short, it has come to designate the *external factor* that was once the manifestation of a man's honor.

In this expanded and sober sense, prestige has entered the vocabulary of sociology. There it is used to designate the empirical fact of social recognition, without any value-judgment being implied. And a distinction is usually made between personality-toned individual prestige and structurally toned social prestige. But its ever more frequent use in everyday speech, as a substitute for the concept of honor, points to a profound change in the social life and class-consciousness of modern man. The pluralistic and open-ended structures of modern societies have eliminated the simplicity and absoluteness of their traditional claims.

Changing Societal Conditions

Examined more closely, this process turns out to be the necessary consequence of a broad-ranging social evolution. Two socio-cultural tendencies seem to be the leading factors in this whole evolution: (1) The rejection of any and every class system based upon a rigid and fixed classification of social honor, and the espousal of "equal opportunity for all" as the precondition for a functional, efficient industrial culture based on the division of labor; (2) The constitutional protection of the individual's chances for social life and advancement by the establishment of equality before the law.

Let us consider the first aspect for a moment. An authoritarian and class-structured society was formed in Europe during the early Middle Ages. Despite deep changes, it prevailed, to some extent, right up to the start of the present century. In it we find a social structure which brought man into a fixed system of interrelationships on the basis of equal rights, equal duties and equal honor. The members of one social class stood over against those of other social classes.

One interesting characteristic of this class-conscious outlook was that it did not feed exclusively on group-centered solidarity and class egoism; in contrast to the modern attitude of class consciousness, which fed on social conflict, the medieval outlook involved some consideration of society as a whole. It involved recognition of other social classes and conscious willingness to fit into the overall hierarchical order that gave substance and legitimacy to one's own social position. One of the central criteria for the whole classification process was the fact and heritage of one's birth; whatever further differentiation might be made on the basis of one's social function or profession, that matter of one's birth remained as a normative criterion of personal dignity and honor.

Such a social system could, in a real sense, satisfy man's need for stability and permanence. It gave him a real feeling of security and class belonging, clearly defining his mode of social existence and giving him "a place to stand" and "room to work in". As the modern emancipation movements and their notions of equality and freedom gained headway, however, the older social system seemed less and less satisfactory. The gradual loss of social and psychological security, which had been provided by the older system, weighed down upon the individual. Henceforth he himself would have to work out his social standing, and he would have to fight for his social prestige in a radically different way.

The older concept of social class was capable of organizing the whole of society into a hierarchical structure and of providing the individual with a well-defined social position. By contrast, the modern social structure lacks any overall ordering principle, for the principle of equal opportunity, as espoused by the modern world, implies that chances for personal advancement are opened up completely and that ideas, needs, opinions and value systems are also open-ended. The chance for personal fulfillment by all is only then given an opportunity to operate, to exert influence, and to become a factor in man's social life.

One result of this process is a pluralistic set of institutions and a wide variety of social groupings, which rules out a macrostructural synthesis of overall social values and classifications. This very pluralism now threatens to relativize the whole concept of honor. As a reaction to this dilemma, there is a growing tendency to use honor, in the sense of real commitment and moral value, only in connection with behavior patterns and social expectations that are of special importance and necessity within a pluralistic society. The numerous other types of social evaluation and class standing are subsumed under the notion of prestige, but this does not mean that the notion of prestige is without moral significance.

While the notion of equal opportunity has become a decisive structuring factor in modern society, it has not become so purely on its intrinsic validity or moral force. The most important influence here has been the radical economic restructuring that resulted from the industrial revolution. It became evident that an industrial society could not operate on the basis of frozen, authoritarian class structures. It would have to operate out of a social order where performance played a key role, and this implied equal opportunity for all. As a result, the concept of *occupation* became a dominant factor in social evaluation within modern industrial cultures; it also became the chief indicator for evaluating the social position of the individual.

A peculiar ambivalence crops up at this juncture. On the one hand, the new industrial cultures provide a host of new occupations and social roles, opening up wide possibilities for individual advancement and prosperity. On the other hand, many occupations cannot provide people with a feeling that they really have an important place in society. They are stuck in "jobs", which are certainly necessary and productive but hardly prestigious. Lack of prestige fosters a tendency to compensate by developing status standards that do not depend upon one's occupation.

Here the criterion may be performance (e.g., in sports) or pre-ethical considerations (e.g., the ownership of luxury goods). Every little variation in dress or living style and every improvement in consumer goods—in short, anything that sets one person off from the common herd—can serve a prestige function. This whole process is given added impetus by a production system that depends on the creation of ever increasing new markets.

This pluralistic outlook on social class and prestige, in which evaluation is based on performance or status symbols or similar external features, necessarily causes a radical change in the moral and psychological attitude of the individual toward his position and place in society. He can no longer subsume all these desirable indicators of status under the old category of honor.

The second factor mentioned above also contributed to the diminishing relevance of honor as a social concept in the minds of men. When the State took over the protection of man's rights and social opportunities by establishing constitutional equality before the law, the protection of a man's honor was no longer a matter for the individual himself. The courts would protect him from slander, and some loss of honor would not put his whole life and social existence in dire jeopardy, as it once did. As a result, honor no longer would have the moral importance it once had.

The ever diminishing ethical content of the concept of honor and the more humanistic means and forms by which it is now protected have certainly contributed to the diminishing relevance of the whole notion of honor. When people come to realize that conflicts can be settled in more satisfactory ways, there is less need to stand upon a point of honor.

National honor—we usually say national prestige today—is also a less acute issue. Economic considerations have led to international agreements and supranational confederations, and the destructive potential of modern warfare has been a major factor in the change. As Behrendt has noted, the only way to preserve freedom today is to give up force as a means of settling conflicts.

Perduring Tieups

The concept of prestige, then, is better suited to express the polyvalence and dynamism of present-day social life than is the traditional notion of honor. Yet it remains a version of the older notion insofar as the latter has basic elements of perduring value. As a result, I would say that the socio-ethical evaluation of prestige is subject to the same criteria as the older notion of honor was, though we must realize that these criteria may need a different focal point of stress today.

I cannot go into a detailed proof of this assertion here,[1] so I shall restrict my analysis to a comparison between the basic criteria that have been used to give moral legitimacy to the notions of honor and prestige respectively. The definitive ethical measurement for honor has been *virtue*. The definitive ethical measurement for presitge has been *accomplishment*.

Classical ethics, from Aristotle on, has held that honor is and should be the "prize of virtue". But here "virtue" should not be taken in the restricted individualistic sense that we give it today. As defined by St. Thomas (*dispositio perfecti ad optimum*), it is something which is indeed tied up with man's inner life and difficult to realize, but as such it continues to remain a disposition toward *what can be realized*. This suggests that we can talk

---

[1] On this whole question, see my book *Ehre, Prestige, Gewissen* (Cologne, 1966).

about virtue whenever man's potential feats are honorable and meritorious, whether it is in the area of personal behavior or of socio-cultural phenomena.

Now this same notion finds echoes in the modern concept of accomplishment. Like virtue (in the classical sense), accomplishment implies the ethical note of achieving and concretely realizing one's potential by personal effort.

A second tieup between virtue and accomplishment comes to light in the motivation and goal-setting that attend every form of human activity. There is a difference in emphasis between them, to be sure, for accomplishment puts much greater stress on the functional. As a result, accomplishment is more readily open to measurement, planning and objective calculation. It is, as it were, the quantitative dimension of qualitative virtue.

The greater suitability of the notion of accomplishment for a pluralistic world is grounded, to a large extent, on the fact that it is quantitative and measurable. In the framework of accomplishment, human activity becomes a usable category that transcends specific cultural contexts and historical stages. Virtue often does not have this advantage.

Seen in this light, prestige is one form of rewarding accomplishment in society. To put it better: accomplishment becomes the determining ethical criterion of prestige. Thus we have set up a normative factor which serves as a critique of any pre-ethical claims to prestige.

In the last analysis, the transition from honor to prestige is the manifestation of a general ethical transformation. It is not just an indication of ethical decline.

PART II
BIBLIOGRAPHICAL
SURVEY

Theo Beemer/*Nijmegen, Netherlands*

The Interpretation of Moral Theology

Today Catholic moral theologians are beginning to accept the terms of theological ethics and Christian ethics in order to describe their particular discipline, as had already been done in the 18th century. J. Rief once entitled a bibliographical survey "Moral Theology or Christian Ethics?" [1] in order to show that questions about the autonomy of man as a moral subject and about his own moral knowledge and moral conduct today receive more attention from the theologians than the discussion of the system of moral norms as such.

The theologians have been led to this because many faithful today have a strong sense of man's moral autonomy. Such believers are of the opinion that moral experience provides them with a reliable understanding of good and evil, and they do not accept that some religious assumption can cast suspicion on this knowledge as being disqualified because obscured by sin, then to be rejected in order to make room for a positive proclamation of God's will or God's law as the norm for man's conduct. To claim such autonomy is not necessarily the same as being self-satisfied or self-opinionated because it can often go together with a keen sense of the dangers that threaten humanity, such as sacrificing human beings to the defense of a system, the harden-

[1] J. Rief, "Moraltheologie oder christliche Ethik? Ein Literaturbericht," in *Theol. Prakt. Quartalschrift* 116 (1968), pp. 59-80.

ing of moral awareness into dogmatism, bad ideology or individualism. The claim is rather directed against a religious or ecclesiastical proclamatoin which pretends that it alone possesses the true knowledge of what is worthy or unworthy of man, what ennobles and what abases him, whatever the sources such a proclamation appeals to.

It is clear that the consciousness of this autonomy is closely linked with the solidarity of all men, Christian or otherwise. Many Christians realize that, together with their contemporaries, they are confronted with identical challenges and identical opportunities. For instance, that the great achievements in space show up the idiocy of unequality, discrimination and injustice among the inhabitants of this planet is evident to all and implies a moral challenge to everyone. Thus, when the Church talks about God's will as the norm of human conduct, this is seen by many either as a superfluous statement of what we already know as good and worth pursuing, a belated confirmation, or as an attempt at breaking through what is experienced by all and setting Christians apart from the rest of mankind as a group of better informed initiates.[2]

I

THE INTERPRETING FUNCTIONS OF MORAL THEOLOGY

This article deals with the function of interpretation in moral theology. By hermeneutics (interpretation) we understand first of all the teaching of the principles which control the interpretation of pronouncements and other texts. The rule here is that one must allow the text to speak for itself and use all appropriate means to ensure this. On the other hand, an essential part is also played by the interpreter's own situation, particularly his own

[2] Cf. J. Stelzenberger, *Zedenleer van het koninkrijk Gods* (1962), p. 24 and *Lehrbuch der Moraltheologie. Die Sittlichkeitslehre der König-sherrschaft Gottes* (Paderborn, 1953) in connection with his opinion about non-Christians.

already existing relatedness to the reality which is brought out in the text; this means that he approaches the text with a particular question of his own, expecting the text to be also addressed to him. Thus the interpretation of historical texts can lead the interpreter to some self-understanding and give an answer to contemporary questions through this confrontation with the text.[3]

1. When we apply this to the interpretation of the Bible as witness to God's revelation and to the believing response which this revelation found in the community of the Old and New Testaments at the time, the problem of interpretation for the faithful is as follows: How must we interrogate and explain the Bible, and how must we interpret the dogmatic tradition as the process of the historical transmission of the faithful's understanding of the Bible, so that the modern believer can hear the voice of God and understand it in his own language?

In theology these hermeneutics develop particularly in relation to the believing interpretation of biblical and dogmatic statements. The importance of this for moral theology is evident when we think of the danger of presenting modern man with something as the will of God, or as a divine command when it is not so in any sense, or in a case where the real will of God can be misunderstood. As an example of the latter case I may mention the way in which moral theology interprets the Sermon on the Mount by referring to the distinction between command and counsel. The Catholic believer accepts that the right interpretation of God's Word can only be found in connection with the whole community of the Church, to whom the Bible was given and where it is read in public. In the Church the Spirit guides the preservation, transmission and proclamation of the apostolic witness, and those charged with the magisterium are competent to provide an authentic, official and public in-

[3] Cf. G. Hasenhüttle, "Die Radikalisierung der hermeneutischen Fragestellung durch Rudolf Bultmann," in *Mysterium Salutis* I (Einsiedeln, 1965), pp. 428-40; E. Schillebeeckx, "Naar een katholiek gebruik van de hermeneutiek," in *Geloof bij kenterend getij* (Roermond, 1967), pp. 78-116.

terpretation as their specific service to the community, occasionally with the guarantee of infallibility.[4]

2. Moral theology, however, is not only concerned with the
interpretation of the Bible and God's call to action as witnessed
and received therein, but must also account for the knowledge
and interpretation of natural morality—i.e., the rational insights
into the value and dignity of the human person, with the consequent demands on human conduct. Moral theology is neither
able nor willing to ignore this source of knowledge, but it has
to examine whether and how the appeal to this knowledge of
good and evil is justified by the tradition of Christian belief.
The Church claims a privileged position with regard to the knowledge and interpretation of what is morally good insofar as this
knowledge cannot be drawn from the revealed Word. Within
the Church the magisterium has claimed the competence to give
an authentic interpretation of this law, while explicitly recog-
nizing that this knowledge is accessible to all men, and that
there is therefore no monopoly. Since Pope Pius IX this claim
has been made increasingly, most recently in the encyclical
Humane Vitae.[5] The argument is that Christ appointed Peter
and the other apostles as the authentic guardians and interpreters of the whole moral law, not only the law of the Gospel but
also the natural law. For the latter, too, is an expression of God's
will, and the faithful observance of this will is man's necessary
way to salvation. Pope Pius XII stressed this competence in
1954, particularly against the opinion that the Church should
not intervene outside the terrain of "strictly religious affairs",
and he pointed out that the observance of the natural moral
law belonged to the way of salvation. The apostles, too, acted
as interpreters of the natural law. This last point suggests that
an examination into the style of moral instruction in the apostolic Church could provide a norm and a clarification for the

[4] Cf. *Constitution on Divine Revelation,* n. 10, with the commentary
by J. Ratzinger, in *Lex. Theol. Kirche* ([2]1967), pp. 526-27.

[5] Pope Paul VI, Encyclical *Humanae Vitae,* nn. 4 and 18. Cf. Pope
Pius XII, Address to Cardinals and Bishops of Nov. 2, 1954, in *A.A.S.* 46
(1954), pp. 671-72.

present problem of ecclesiastical intervention in the field of morality.

Natural moral law is then proposed by the Church as an expression of God's will. The term "interpretation" suggests comparison of the natural law to a given text or a code of law that can be read. Thus we meet again the hermeneutical problem of how to voice the demands of human dignity in such a way that the faithful of today can somehow hear there the voice of God.

3. Finally, moral theology is also faced with the task of interpreting the "signs of the times". The Church, conscious of her place in the history of mankind, has declared in the conciliar *Pastoral Constitution of the Church in the Modern World* that she "has always had the duty of scrutinizing the signs of the times and of interpreting them in the light of the Gospel".[6] This rich expression is developed in article 11 of the same Constitution: "Motivated by this faith, the People of God labors to decipher authentic signs of God's presence and purpose in the happenings, needs and desires in which this People has a part along with other men of our age. For faith throws a new light on everything, manifests God's design for man's total vocation, and thus directs the mind to solutions which are fully human." Here, once more, we need hermeneutics, now related to the "reading" and "explanation" not of texts, but of events and experiences. Here, too, the rule holds that the events must not be twisted to suit the interpreter (who is in fact a prophet), but listened to and interrogated so that in the prevailing events, aspirations and needs a call from God may be discerned. F. Furger[7] has pointed out that the Council did not relate this understanding of the signs of the times to individual morality but to the social problems of our age. He nevertheless maintains that the individual must also read these signs in order to discover what good he must do as a responsible member of his society and what the will of God means to him in this field. This

---

[6] *Constitution on the Church in the Modern World*, n. 4.
[7] F. Furger, "Prudence and Moral Change," in *Concilium* 35 (1968), pp. 129f.

interpretation therefore belongs without any doubt to the hermeneutical function of moral theology. It is interesting that Karl
Rahner has used the terms of his "formal existential ethics" for
the interpretation of the Pastoral Constitution.

II

HERMENEUTICS AS THE SCIENCE OF "UNDERSTANDING"

Insofar as moral theology belongs to the science of theology, it shares in the hermeneutical problems of theology, and we
can describe its particular form of interpretation provisionally as
the science of the faithful interpretation of Scripture, the dogmatic tradition, the natural moral law and the signs of the times
in order to draw from these sources an understanding of the
will of God as the norm for our conduct. But the moral
theologian is and remains primarily a student of ethics. He is
therefore caught up in the tension between the Church's proclamation of the religious message about God and his giving and
demanding will on the one hand, and man's moral experiences,
achievements and aspirations, both past and present, on the
other. As a student of ethics he is more familiar with the ethical
categories of good and evil, just and unjust, *honestum* and
inhonestum, than with the religious categories of sin and holiness,
salvation and damnation.

And here we meet a truly hermeneutical problem: How does
man's self-understanding as an ethical subject (leaving aside
whether this self-understanding is seen as a search for human
authenticity, for self-development, for identity, for love or for
a better world) fit in with the understanding of God's revelation
in Jesus Christ as the foundation, motive or norm for human
conduct? Does the faith justify and seriously accept the autonomy
of ethical thinking? And, inversely, does ethical awareness and
seriousness pave the way for a true understanding of God's
Word as a promise and appeal addressed to us, so that we

understand the death and resurrection of Jesus as important and liberating for us?

Rather than concentrate on the problems given to moral theology by Scripture, tradition, natural law and the signs of the times, I want to deal here with this hermeneutical question of the relation between the language and categories of ethical awareness and those of the Christian proclamation. It is useful to remember here that both kinds of concepts contain a sociological reference: the first refers to human societies, the history of ethics as part of cultural history, the way in which modern man is aware of his responsibility for mankind's continuity (cf. the expression "survival ethics") and future, while the second refers to the Church as a group within which people discuss the will of God in proclamation and theology as seen in their own tradition and history.

III
How To Reconcile Ethics and Faith?

1. In various studies [8] C. van Ouwerkerk has stressed that the "theological" (here meaning "directed toward God") dimension of moral and immoral conduct is far from obvious. It is not easy to see this point. We are wont to speak about the will of God expressed in the order of creation. According to van Ouwerkerk, it is therefore understandable that we cling to an idea of the will of God as creator and legislator, because in this theistic perspective the relation between "the moral order" and God becomes clear and almost tangible. Thus, in moral theology, arguing on metaphysical lines, we see moral goodness as a given participation in the fullness of God's being and goodness, and the moral obligation to self-realization is more

[8] C. van Ouwerkerk, "Gospel Morality and Human Compromise," in *Concilium* 5 (1965), pp. 7f.; "Christus en de ethiek," in *Tijdschr. v. Theol.* 6 (1966), pp. 307-17; "Secularism and Christian Ethics," in *Concilium* 25 (1967), pp. 83f.

closely defined as a task and an appeal imposed by the creating
God through consideration of the relation between creator and
creature. This gives the impression that man, by acting "according to reason" or "against reason", declares himself for or
against God, is obedient or disobedient, loses or gains his soul,
without his decision being affected by God's historical entry
into human life and the communion offered by God's grace
in Jesus Christ. The "short cut" from the "moral order" to
the creative will of God, suggested by theism, does not explain,
for instance, how moral misconduct such as slander, maltreat-
ment, fraudulent tax returns or debauchery can be a sin—i.e., a
rejection or ignoring of God's love as it meets us in history.[9]
Hence a theological approach will always have to stress that the
relation between ethics and the acceptance and fulfillment of
God's will can only be witnessed to in faith, not pointed out
with a finger, and that an "identification" can only come about
through the process of history. Here God's will must then be
understood as his saving will, manifesting itself in its giving,
liberating and questioning action in man's history, and there
understood as such.

Van Ouwerkerk's thesis that "the connection between our
moral goodness in this world and salvation is not transparent" [10]
excludes, properly understood, two other theses: (a) this connection *is* transparent, and thus there is an easy and direct
identification between ethics and faith; (b) there is no connection, and therefore our responsible actions in the world, our
search for what is right, for more humanity and peace, receive
no strength, support or critical discernment from our belief in
God. (This attitude could not accept Jesus as an example or
teacher of humanity.)

Van Ouwerkerk's own position becomes gradually less clear
in his studies. At first he pointed to love of neighbor as the

[9] Cf. the ecclesiastical condemnation of the doctrine of the *peccatum
philosophicum seu morale* (philosophical or moral sin), August 24, 1960
(DS 2291).

[10] "Gospel Morality . . .", *art. cit.,* p. 14.

link between moral goodness and justification through faith, but he also thought that, in order to find out what this love asks of us, we are referred back to the world and its changing and unstable notions about good and evil.[11] Elsewhere he formulates the problem in terms of interpretation: Can we say that the kerygma merely reinterprets man's moral goodness as salvation or does it have its own ethical message to the world, even with regard to content? [12] In the first case, faith interprets the ethics toward which man gropes (by looking at them as a matter of what is good and humane), and testifies that those who do "such things" will inherit the kingdom of God. Here one wonders whether such a reinterpretation does not exclude any opportunity for criticism so that the proclamation would be limited to a pronouncing of God's blessing on the historical results achieved by man's "natural" moral knowledge.

2. In W. van der Marck's work on fundamental morality [13] the relation between morality in this world and communion with God lies in the realm of knowledge. The function of the Christian proclamation is to interpret. It unveils what has been the reality "from the beginning"—namely, God's presence in all that is human. "God's incarnation and his presence in humanity cannot be demonstrated by historical investigation, but is a fact, a truth and a reality of salvation from the foundation of the world, and man cannot see it until God has opened his eyes to it." [14] The proclamation concerning Christ shows forth creation as incarnation and redemption. Hence any ethic is of necessity a Christian ethic, and a human ethic is in fact a Christian ethic. The result is that we only practice a truly Christian ethic when we constantly and consistently recognize man's autonomy and recognize it effectively.[15] In the unfolding of this thesis, the essential intersubjectivity of all human action

---

[11] In *Tijdschr. v. Theol.*, *art. cit.*, p. 316.

[12] "Secularism . . .", *art. cit.*, pp. 107 and 138.

[13] W. H. M. van der Marck, *Het Christusgeheim in de menselijke samenleving. Hoofdlijnen van een christelijke ethiek* (Roermond, 1966).

[14] *Op. cit.*, p. 28.

[15] *Op. cit.*, p. 26.

displays the shape of God's presence in the world. Thus human intersubjectivity becomes communion with God.[16]

In this view it is the kerygma which itself fully justifies the autonomy of the moral subject, of human ethics, and of the way man knows and lives his humanity. The person who accepts the proclamation of Christ learns to understand himself as someone who, by realizing the potentialities bestowed on him as a creature, attains salvation because God offers man his saving presence in these very potentialities. Intersubjectivity belongs to the "nature" of the human act, as well as the purposive (*agere propter finem*) and rational character of the act. In this intersubjectivity lies the offer of communion with God (*beatitudo*). Hence a good action is identical with the achievement of intersubjectivity (humanity), and this is in fact identical with the recognition of God and communion with God. The proclamation of Christ reveals this truth, so that christology contains the hermeneutic of ethics: thus man is shown what was hidden from the foundation of the world.

The purpose of van der Marck's book is to show, by some basic thinking, how essential the link is between the proclamation of Christ and giving or refusing one's fellow man something to eat or drink, between a life that tends toward God and the everyday humanity anywhere in the world through which man attains salvation; in fact, they coincide.

We seem to find here, however, a certain ambiguity in the way the author speaks of intersubjectivity; it is described as a quality of the human act, and not as an event, a relationship between two persons. No account is taken of the factual and historical appearance of one man in the life of another, nor of the inevitable recognition which is still present in the antagonism of man's selfishness. Nor are we told whether and how one man reaches the other effectively. Connected with this is the absence of the category of historicity (also in christology). It is not shown anywhere that history is important for man's self-understanding and self-realization. One wonders whether the

---

[16] *Op. cit.*, pp. 55 and 58.

mysterious truth that every man can be justified before God and serve Christ through the everyday practice of neighborly love is adequately explained by reflecting upon the moral equipment (with the addition of God's ever present offer of salvation) given to man in his rational nature, and therefore given to all, everywhere and always, without bringing in the personal and historical categories of "I" and "you", of past, present and future, of "events" (different from "accidents") and history.

3. When we continue our search for an explanation of the relation between ethics and faith, goodness and justification, moral duty and God's will, the moral theologian can also consult the traditional teaching that every man, living in ignorance of the Gospel, can be justified before God by his moral conduct as guided by "the law written on his heart" (Rom. 2, 15). When the *Constitution on the Church* [17] talks about the various ways in which people are related to salvation and God's People, it says that "those also can attain to everlasting salvation who through no fault of their own do not know the Gospel of Christ or his Church, yet sincerely seek God and, moved by grace, strive by their deeds to do his will as it is known to them through the dictates of conscience". The same is said of "those who, without blame on their part, have not yet arrived at an explicit knowledge of God, but who strive to live a good life, thanks to his grace". The distinction between these two social categories seems to lie between those who consciously seek the "unknown God" in shadows and images (in nature, particularly in the human person or in the community, or in history, as J. Grillmeier observes), and the theoretical "atheists". But both have in common that they can find the God of salvation if they follow their moral conscience and lead a good life. How this justifying encounter with God comes about is not said, but it is difficult to accept that this "conversion" falls outside the guidance of the conscience and outside the context of a good life. We find an indication in the *Pastoral Constitution on the Church in the Modern World*

---

[17] *Constitution on the Church*, n. 16 with commentary by J. Grillmeier, in *Lex. Theol. Kirche* ([2]1966), pp. 205-07.

where it mentions the moral conscience: "In a wonderful manner, conscience reveals that law which is fulfilled by love of God and of neighbor." [18] We can therefore try to understand this "anonymous" approach to, and acceptance of, the God of salvation by using ethical categories instead of the religious ones so often used in the past. What the conciliar text describes as the lowest degree of man's relationship to the People of God can then perhaps be seen as the first degree of the Christian's relationship to mankind and the world.

First of all, we may in general terms refer to the well-known theory of "anonymous Christianity" and its later developments. Starting with the postulate of God's universal will of salvation, theology came to accept a universal history of salvation which is co-extensive with the history of the world. When this term "universal history of salvation" is used, we must add the qualification that it does not totally correspond to the concept of history, because, although it refers to events and free decisions, it does not show the visible and public continuity in these events.[19] What is important from the ethical point of view is not so much the application of this theory to non-Christian religions, as to the relationships and encounters between man and man.

It is curious that moral theologians have taken no or very little part in the development of this theory. I will now refer here to some of the many studies that have appeared.

J. Ratzinger [20] warns against opinions which, for all practical purposes, hold that good will is a sufficient principle of salvation for one half of mankind. When we look to the New Testament for an answer to the question as to what man must have in actual fact in order to be a "Christian", we find two answers, and these complement each other. The first is that he who has love has all. Not the knowledge of the name of the Lord but the "human" treatment of God hidden in man is what saves man. But over

[18] *Constitution on the Church in the Modern World*, n. 16.
[19] Cf. A. Darlap, "Fundamentale Theologie der Heilsgeschichte," in *Mysterium Salutis* I (Einsiedeln, 1965), pp. 3-156 (esp. pp. 80-90).
[20] J. Ratzinger, "Salus extra Ecclesiam nulla est," in *Veranderd Kerkbewustzijn* (Hilversum, 1965), pp. 18-30.

against this we have the plain fact that nobody really possesses love. Our love is constantly infected and twisted by our egotism. This is clear from the double meaning in our use of the terms "human" and "humanity".[21] Man therefore needs an attitude which makes him receptive to the gift of the Lord's vicarious love, and Paul calls this attitude "faith". Even where this attitude does not explicitly refer to Christ, something like a "faith in faith" can exist. This attitude is not a vague good will but can be described as a rejection of complacency and self-righteousness, that simplicity of heart which the Bible describes as "poverty of the spirit".

The second answer then is that faith is enough. But love and faith indicate a tendency to go beyond oneself, where man begins to abandon his egotism (even in his humanitarianism or philanthropy) and to go out to the other man. Thus we find in our fellow man the primary indication of "God incognito" whenever the presence of our fellow man helps us in this saving "exodus" from our own self.[22] Ratzinger points out that God can also choose other "incognitos" and that various religious or mundane facts can bring man to invoke help in this process of self-abandonment. But it is equally clear that there are also things which can never represent "God incognito". It is therefore not true that each one can live by his own convictions and is saved by tenaciously clinging to them. Otherwise the perverse obedience or the fanatical courage of an SS man would become a kind of wish to belong to the Church (*votum Ecclesiae*). Man is certainly not saved by the mere conscientious obedience to a system, even if this system has noble features, such as the great religions of the world. For the system always tends toward particularism, toward exclusion and therefore toward an attitude of "over against each other". God, however, does not call us to this "over against" but to that "for" each other, which the Bible calls *agape*. The statement that everyone must live according to his con-

---

[21] In modern religious writings adjectives like "true", "authentic", "radical", "disinterested", "unconditional" are used with "humanity", like a kind of incantation.

[22] Cf. St. Thomas, *Summa Theol.* Ia-IIae, q. 5, a. 5, ad 1m.

science must therefore be qualified. The "dictate of conscience" is not arbitrary and does not tell each of us something different; it tells all of us only this one thing: Love without self-righteousness. This basic attitude turns many a pagan into an "anonymous Christian" and many a Christian into a pseudonymous pagan.

I have given Ratzinger's opinion somewhat extensively because it penetrates deep into the field of ethics and points to realities within our ethical existence in this world. The danger of Pelagianism or of reducing Christian belief to ethics appears not to lie in the emphasis on ethical practice but rather on a superficial, unrealistic and unhistorical reflection on human relations, and also in the identification of one's conscience with one's convictions. These reflections open up a vast field for ethical and cultural-historical investigations which would be of great interest to the theologian. One could think of a wide variety of topics: universalism and particularism (individualism) in ethical, social or religious systems; the inclusive or exclusive life within the institutionalized forms of human society—family, nation, church; the dialectic of what is "familiar" and what is "strange," and our attitude toward the latter; other peoples seen as God's enemies in the Old Testament, and also as enemies of "Christianity"; the idea that God or some saint should take sides in a conflict between nations; the myth of the "good savage" in a European's attitude toward a non-European. The conflict between people and between groups of people, which may lead to alienation as well as to redemption, cannot be ignored by theology.[23] Paul Ricoeur, who tried to construct a theology of love that was at the same time a theology of history, on the basis of a meditation on the "image of God",[24] has pointed to the "iconoclastic" and

[23] In this connection the anthropological assumptions contained in the *Constitution on the Church in the Modern World* have been criticized by F. Houtart and F. Hambye in "Socio-Political Implications of Vatican Council II," in *Concilium* 36 (1968), pp. 85-96.

[24] P. Ricoeur, "L'image de Dieu et l'épopée humaine," in *Histoire et vérité* (Paris, ²1964), pp. 112-31; in the same volume also cf. "Le socius et le prochain" (pp. 99-111).

"scandalizing" function of literature and art as enabling us to break through the collective presuppositions we have about humanity. It is precisely the believing recognition of a justification and sanctification on the basis of existential moral practice which makes it necessary to investigate extensively the problems created by the mutual acceptance and avoidance among human beings and the many ways in which these problems arise.

Ratzinger shows that his definition of the subjective components of salvation already imply the objective factor, for in every kind of human love we can see an essential deficiency which makes it inadequate in the eyes of God. That is why we need the vicarious service of Jesus Christ, without which the receptive gesture of the "faith" (*pistis*), the simplicity of a heart which knows its own abysmal failings, would be pointless.[25] This, too, links up with our moral experience: a moral life not only needs the moral imperative that the good *must* be done, but also the confidence that the good *can* be done, and in fact is seen to be done. And here we should draw attention to the structure and function of the example and the paradigm, to which far too little attention has been paid by fundamental moral theology. The human subject, aware of man's abysmal failings (and this awareness does not need preaching about "sin"), asks himself whether the good really exists, whether love and dialogue between human beings is possible, whether universal peace is attainable, whether human beings can ultimately reach each other, or perhaps only in a small circle to the exclusion of others, and if so, whether results can be made to last. Such a man, who nevertheless tries to explain himself to himself, will then turn to Jesus Christ as the Lord. The heart of the Christian confession, "Jesus Christ is the Lord", says that love between men does exist, that it has been shown to exist and that it has opened a future based on it, even beyond death, so that it is not forever consigned to oblivion. Elsewhere Ratzinger has made the plea that all theology, moral theology included, should be above all a theology of the

[25] *Loc. cit.*, p. 48.

resurrection.[26] This concept of theology, based on salvation history, brings with it a well-defined program of reflection on the phenomenon of human relationships in their social and historical dimensions.

B. Willems [27] has tried to make the mystery of redemption by Christ intelligible to us through the mystery of the other human person. Why, he asks, should one man not be allowed to assume complete control over "objectify" or manipulate another man? There is ultimately no other reason than the experience that the other man, too, manifests and embodies that transcendent other, who is God. Redemption is then described as allowing the other to meet us precisely as "other" (i.e., as both strange and similar to us). This demands a change in us which the Bible calls *metanoia*, conversion. At first man experiences this as a loss to himself because he feels it as a deprivation of his autonomy. Through the "grace" of the other, however, man rediscovers himself, and only then are that true freedom and creativeness experienced which are no longer possessiveness but a respect which enlarges the scope of his personality. The most concrete revelation of God is the other man by my side. The offer of salvation has been given shape in a unique way in the life, death and resurrection of Jesus of Nazareth. In him, "the other" meets us.

There are points here which correspond to Ratzinger's vision. However, Willems is only partially successful in explaining the relation between Christ's redemptive act as "offer" and our present redemption as "communion". The reason is perhaps that this communion is seen too much in personal terms so that mankind and its history are not envisaged. The cultural image of man, which has inserted itself in all relationships as the true relationship between one man and another, and which is just as much in need of renewal, is not really taken into consideration. Moreover, the relation between man and Christ is seen mainly in the

---

[26] J. Ratzinger, "Heilsgeschichte und Eschatologie. Zur Frage nach dem Ansatz des theologischen Denkens," in *Theologie im Wandel* (Munich, 1967), pp. 68-69.

[27] B. Willems, *De verlossing in kerk en wereld* (Roermond, 1967).

light of an interpersonal encounter, so that the faith is not related to someone who has become the "image" or "type" of man, the figure of a man who is both himself and all mankind.[28]

K. Rahner's study of the act of neighborly love as the original relation between man and God [29] also contributes to our problem of the connection between ethical and religious categories. The loving relationship between two people is not just one existential act, side by side with other equivalent ones, but the real and all-embracing act in man's existence. In this original act, God is there as the ground of this experience, not as the immediate object but "indirectly". Even when God is seen in the religious category, when he himself speaks and becomes man's partner, this always happens in a man who is already "of this world", already aware of his "self" through personal encounter and communication with the "you" of experience. Inversely, the love which stakes itself in the unconditional acceptance of the other man is always already a love which includes the love of God. God's speaking in salvation history, which makes it possible for us to recognize our relation to him, always presupposes love among men. When man therefore addresses himself to God in an explicit act of knowledge and love, this is a secondary act which derives from and rests on the original experience of God in human communication. The neighbor is not loved first of all because God wills or prescribes it; the act of neighborly love, springing from grace, is itself a love which is open to God. In the free decision to take the neighbor wholly seriously, God is recognized, even when man cannot articulate this experience of God for himself. That is why the final judgment is apparently given on the basis of wholly atheistic norms (Mt. 25, 31-46). The love of Jesus Christ (i.e., toward Jesus Christ) is the unique and highest act of neighborly love, and yet the most sublime deed toward Jesus is still founded on the presupposition of the every-

[28] Cf. P. Ricoeur, *Finitude et Culpabilité. II. La symbolique du mal* (Paris, 1960), pp. 243-60.

[29] K. Rahner, *Warum und wie können wir die Heiligen verehren?* (Einsiedeln, 1966), pp. 283-303.

day love toward the other man. Only he who has already met
Christ incognito in his brother and sister can meet Christ openly
and explicitly.

There are some important indications here for our problem: in
concrete life, the act of human communion (which in Rahner's
view certainly implies a free acceptance of grace) is the necessary condition for the understanding of a category which we
describe as the "will of God". Rahner does not say by what kind
of explicit motive this human love is inspired; and if this act is
the fulfillment of a law or command, it is not true love. Is it then
not under the command of conscience and a fulfillment of natural moral law? This can only be affirmed if one does not see the
moral imperative, recognized by the conscience, as an obligation
but primarily as an invitation and encouragement, and natural
moral law not as an order to be obeyed but as a directive found
in personal experience. On these conditions one may say that the
voice which calls man to the bold venture of love is more "original" and can be seen as the will of God, as it is known from
the historical revelation. We can understand the will of God as
the rule for human conduct only through the actual and effective
practice of neighborly love, guided by "natural" moral knowledge.

4. Can moral theology work with what it has learned about
the practice of a moral life as the way of salvation? Traditional
Catholic moral theology has recognized the order of creation
also as an objective source of knowledge of God's will, side by
side with the word of revelation. But can these two be put simply
on the same level? J. Kraus [30] thinks that the problems for moral
theology do not lie so much in the legitimacy of this natural
source of knowledge and the recognition of its relative autonomy
as in their mutual relationship. The basic significance of natural
moral knowledge lies in the fact that it lays the foundation for
moral duty, binding us to opt for the good. Man recognizes that
his existence involves a "must", and only in this way can he see

[30] J. Kraus, "Um die Wissenschaftlichkeit der Moraltheologie," in
Freib. Zeitschr. f. Phil. Theol. 13/14 (1966-67), pp. 23-46.

himself as a being that is subject to obedience to God and his Word. B. Schüller [31] understands the natural moral awareness as the transcendental presupposition (the necessary precondition) for the understanding of Christ's moral message. The believing understanding of this message is only possible for him who already sees himself as subject to natural moral law.

In the light of what has already been said, these statements can be developed in two ways. First of all, natural moral awareness is the necessary pre-condition for understanding the kerygma and the notion of "God's will". The common statement that the will of God can be known from the order of creation is itself already a statement of belief. As such it is based on the understanding of the moral good *qua* good, and not as the "will of God". Secondly, we may ask whether the moral awareness of being bound to do the good is enough by itself to understand God's will as will-to-salvation, or whether this also requires a certain moral practice, a personal experience.

5. E. Simons [32] has made an interesting observation about the central role played by the human encounter, with its historical and social circumstances, in man's understanding of himself and of revelation. His argument proceeds on the lines of existential philosophy: What links the discovery of the truth of my self-understanding with the understanding of revelation, and how does this link come about historically? For him, the central point is that the hermeneutical problem can only be fully grasped in the dialogue, the encounter of two people who understand each other. This "understanding each other" is a happening in which two people not only come to understand themselves but experience at the same time what "understanding" really means. Dialogue is a hermeneutical event, and there is an awareness of this in it. Thus the dialogue is the key to the hermeneutical problem; it creates access to the word of truth which itself is shared between people in a history of transmission. The dialogical

[31] B. Schüller, "Zur theologischen Diskussion über die lex naturalis," in *Theol. u. Phil.* 41 (1966), pp. 481-503.

[32] E. Simons, "Die Bedeutung der Hermeneutik für die katholische Theologie," in *Catholica Mstr.* 21 (1967), pp. 184-212.

understanding of the word of salvation is rooted in the dialogue relationship between persons, and this relationship entails not only an "understanding" but also a moral decision.

In recent years many theologians have turned to the historical, social and political implications of man's existence, with the result that they have begun to see that the search for and discovery of identity cannot be limited to personal relationship but also requires the search for a "new humanity" in the creation of a social order. The formation of morality, the cultural formation of the image of what is "worthy of man", is then seen as an unceasing attempt at discovering in which direction God's creative purpose lies and setting it out in certain norms of conduct without ever being able to turn it into an ideology or a system. The guidance of the conscience which urges man to know and practice truly human values is shown in the course of history not only in the developing ethos but also in the equally constant criticism of this ethos in the name of a more universal recognition of man's true worth. In this connection E. Schillebeeckx [33] speaks of a "contrast experience" which leads to protest, hope, promise and historical intiative.

IV

THE INTERPRETING FUNCTION OF THE CHURCH

The Church's task with regard to the common search for the truth of humanity lies primarily in the proclamation that it is possible to be human. The Church draws this proclamation from Scripture. This Scripture is not a textbook of moral principles. Taken as a whole, Scripture leads us to the knowledge of God's covenant with the people of Israel and all other peoples. It tells us to order human society on the basis of our confidence that God has deigned to live among us and to create peace.

The use of Scripture in the Church and in moral theology cre-

[33] E. Schillebeeckx, "The Magisterium and the World of Politics," in *Concilium* 36 (1968), pp. 19f.

ates a special problem when it comes to finding moral rules.[34] We see how in Israel and in the apostolic age the natural ethos was taken from the current culture and subsumed under the proclamation of the belief in Yahweh, or the life "in Christ", in order to shape the life of the believing community at that time. This process was bound to affect the evolution of the cultural ethos in turn. It is also interesting to see that the early ecclesiastical authors followed Philo and distinguished, within the Torah, between ritual, civil and moral commands, and only considered the last as enduring and universal because they already live in every human heart. Thus the "natural" moral evidence of that time became a kind of selective principle.[35] And are we not doing the same today when, in our interpretation of the Old and the New Testaments, we distinguish between norms that are conditioned by culture and therefore antiquated, on the one hand, and permanent norms on the other?

The Church also gives moral guidance by interpreting natural moral law. This is often understood as the "reading" of a once established order, as if it were a book (the book of nature) or a building plan. This is clear from the frequent references by the magisterium to a "moral order instituted by God" or "defined by God beforehand" (*a Deo praefinitus*), not only in *Humanae Vitae* but also in the *Constitution on the Church in the Modern World*. This of course leads to the criticism of a "cosmic predeterminism". But the same function can also be understood as a critical guidance of the historical ethos of the world by accepting, stimulating and correcting things in the light of the belief in the inalienable value of every human person before God. This also means a belief in the inadequacy of every image or idea of humanity compared with the one image of man given us by God

---

[34] Cf. E. Hamel, "L'usage de l'Ecriture Sainte en théologie morale," in *Gregorianum* 47 (1966), pp. 53-85; also cf. J. Blank, "Does the New Testament Provide Principles for Modern Moral Theology?" in *Concilium* 25 (1967), pp. 9-22, and F. Böckle, "Was ist das Proprium einer christlichen Ethik?" in *Zeitschr. f. Evang. Ethik* 11 (1967), pp. 148-59.

[35] Cf. P. Delhaye, *Le décalogue et sa place dans la morale chrétienne* (Brussels-Paris, 1963).

and to be manifested at the end of time. This way of conceiving the interpretation of natural law comes closer to the interpretation of the signs of the times. It means a shift from doctrinaire language to a more pastoral language [36] and transfers the need for necessary scientific information from the science of quasi-universal laws to the analysis of situations. A good example of this is *Populorum Progressio*.

V

CONCLUSION

Moral theology shows in its own way the hermeneutical circle: the autonomous—or, rather, "dialogue"—practice of morality, taking place in the present under the guidance of the "law" written on man's heart, serves as a preparation for the Gospel, and so enables us to understand the proclamation of God-with-us, God's saving will. Thus, for example, the scriptural message about sexuality can only become valid for us with the help of our understanding today of the meaning of sexuality. The belief in God's saving will, however, makes us see that we do not yet know what is "human", and that we do not know definitely what "good" means. Thus it directs our creative and effective imagination to the appearance of the man who frees our understanding of what is human from the darkness of ambiguity in which this understanding is still imprisoned. The full meaning of human brotherhood, the unity of mankind or the city of God is still beyond our moral imagining, and yet the way in which people today are open to each other or to the drama of human events and experiences is a sign of the coming fulfillment.

Love without self-righteousness as the central act of man's history implies criticism of the ethical categories (the good) and also of religion (the sacred).

[36] K. Rahner, *Zur theologischen Problematik einer "Pastoralkonstitution"* (Einsiedeln, 1967), pp. 613-36.

PART III
DOCUMENTATION
CONCILIUM

Office of the Executive Secretary
Nijmegen, Netherlands

Concilium General Secretariat/*Nijmegen, Netherlands*

Revolution in the Universities: The Moral Problem

Speaking about the situation of scientists (in the broadest sense) in the United States, Albert Einstein said in 1954: "If, as a young man, I again had the choice of how to earn my livelihood, I would not dream of becoming a scientist, scholar or lecturer. I'd rather be a tinker or a peddler in the hope of enjoying a modest measure of independence insofar as this still exists in present circumstances." [1]

The lack of professional freedom in modern society has already been dealt with under various angles in this volume. This sense of lack of freedom now also besets what used to be considered the bulwark of freedom and autonomy, the university. The intention of this article is not to give an exhaustive summary of all the explosions of this feeling in the present unrest at universities. Such a survey can be found elsewhere. The point is rather to

[1] H. Jäckel, "Keine Angst vor der Freiheit der Wissenschaft—Universität und Revolution," in *Frankfurter Hefte* 24 (Feb. 1969), p. 85.

[2] Among others, see R. Neyhaus and F. Steiner, *Dokumente zur Hochschulreform 1945-1959* (Wiesbaden, 1961); S. Leibfried, *Wider die Untertanenfabrik. Handbuch zur Demokratisierung der Hochschule* (Cologne, 1967); idem, *Die angepasste Universität. Zur Situation der Hochschulen in der Bundesrepublik und den U.S.A.* (Frankfurt, 1968); S. M. Lipset, *Student Politics* (New York, 1967); *The University in Time of Change* (Santiago, 1965); R. Anrieu, *Les communistes et la révolution*

look at the moral problems which have emerged in these revolutions. It is obvious that there are here new moral problems because these revolutions erupt on the dividing line between a vanishing culture and a new culture still in the process of formation. All these problems center around the moral exercise of freedom. Freedom is here understood not as the free or obstructed participation in such revolutions, but rather as the task of a

(Paris, 1968); P. Andro, A. Dauvergne, L. M. Lacoutte, *Le Mai et la révolution* (Paris, 1968); J. Sauvageot, D. Cohn Bendit, J. Duteuil and others, *La révolte étudiante* (Paris, 1968); J. J. Servan Schreiber, *Le réveil de la France: mai-juin 1968* (Paris, 1968); B. Revesz, "D'une prise de la Sorbonne à l'autre," in *Terre entière* (May-Aug. 1968); Epistemon (pseudonym of a professor of Nanterre), *Ces idées qui ont ébranlé la France: Nanterre novembre 1967-juin 1968* (Paris, 1968); special issue of *Esprit* (May-June 1964); "La réforme de l'enseignement," *ibid.,* (June 1954); "Les enseignants et la réforme," *ibid.* (Sept. 1968); "Origine et sens du mouvement," *ibid.* (June-July, 1968); G. de Rosa, "Universitari in agitazione," in Civiltà Catolica 119, (March 1968), pp. 593-95; N. F., "La protesta dei Giovani," in Il Gallo 22 (May 1968), pp. 12-16; G. Melis, "Mao contra i giovani," in Civiltà Catolica 119 (Nov. 1968), pp. 347-60; J. M. de Llanos, "La Iglesia en la revolución de mayo," in *Iglesia viva* 16 (July-Oct. 1968), pp. 369-74; *idem,* "La revolución de mayo," in *Razón y Fe* 850 (Nov. 1968), pp. 378-89; P. Hebblethwaite, "Tsechische Studenten sagen ihre Meinung," in Stimmen der Zeit 93 (June 1968), pp. 407-13; J. Barzun, *The American University: How It Runs, Where It Is Going* (New York, 1968); J. Ridgeway, *The Closed Corporation: American Universities in Crisis* (New York, 1968); F. B. Gomez and L. Martinez, "Seminar on Student Problems in Southeast Asian Universities," in *Philippina Sacra* 3 (Jan.-April 1968), pp. 177-89; R. Braun, "Un grave conflicto en la Universidad Catolica de Cuyo," in *Criterio* V (June 1968), pp. 350-51; C. Castellano, "Invito a un dibattiti sulle 'rivolte dei giovani'," in *Il Gallo* 22 (Oct. 1968), pp. 13-14; F. van den Bussche, "Leuven en de landelijke crisis in België," in *Wending* 23 (March 1968), pp. 57-64; L. van Bladel, "Revolte om Leuven: een ethische verantwoording," in *Streven* 21 (March 1968), pp. 531-39; M. Beloff, "October for the Rebels: Student Barricades in Britain," in *Encounter* 31 (1968), pp. 48-56; J. Alberdi, "La Universidad autonoma," in *Razón y Fe* 850 (Nov. 1968), pp. 304-09; "Les manifestations d'étudiants—Lettre de l'épiscopat polonais au gouvernement," in *La Doc. Catholique* 50 (May 1968), pp. 805-07; "Studentenschaft und Hochschulgemeinden der DDR," in *Herder Korrespondenz* 22 (1968), pp. 312-15; N. Moltschanow, "Westliche Studentenrebellion in sowjetischer Sicht," in *Literaturnaja gazeta* (Nov. 6, 1968) and *Orientierung* 33 (Jan. 1969), pp. 10-12; I. Errera, "Mei 1968: de terechtstelling," in *Wending* 23 (Jan. 1969), pp. 794-814.

group united around human knowledge to ensure for it the freedom it needs in order to exist at all.[3]

If we therefore mention ethics in connection with the revolutionary movement in the universities, we are obviously dealing with what is called macro-ethics (on a large scale), and not with the moral opinions or conduct of individual persons. Much individual good will and responsibility has been paralyzed by immoral collective structures. One of the aims of the university revolution is precisely to expose the immorality of these structures which have deprived the university of its freedom and independence. The question then arises what influence a Christian ethic, based on the Christian view of truth and science, can exercise on these social trends. Something similar was done for the ethics of peace and development in the encyclicals *Pacem in Terris* and *Populorum Progressio*,[4] and in this connection Pope John XXIII referred to the problems connected with the choice of career and education.

For various reasons we have preferred the term "university revolution" to others such as "students' revolt". The first reason is that this revolution is not so much concerned with students, professors or the administration of the university, but rather with the mutual functioning of these three factors and their relation-

[3] W. D. Marsch, "Utopie der Befreiung und christliche Freiheit. Theologischer Versuch über Herbert Marcuse," in *Pastoraltheologie* 58 (Jan. 1969), pp. 17-34. The State guarantees the freedom of science but cannot interpret the idea of science, just as it guarantees the freedom of the Church without being able to define the "Church". This is a constantly recurring aspect of the conflict and can be traced back to the oldest editions of K. Jaspers, *Die Idee der Universität*. Cf. K. Jaspers and K. Rossman, *Die Idee der Universität* (Berlin, 1961), p. 28.

[4] E. Schillebeeckx, "The Magisterium and the World of Politics," in *Concilium* 36 (1968), pp. 19-39; cf. Vatican Council II's *Declaration on Christian Education* with its commentary by M. Plate in *Die Autorität der Freiheit* III (Munich, 1967), pp. 360-66, and the description of this declaration as *superanda* (to be overcome) by H. Kittel, *ibid.*, pp. 367-75. An historical survey of the Church's attitude toward the university and science can be found in R. Lavocat, *L'église et la communauté scientifique internationale. Aventures et conditions d'un dialogue* (Paris, 1965); for a more fundamental treatment, see A. G. Weiler and others, *Leven, weten, geloven* (Hilversum, 1968).

ship with society. The revolution is therefore not satisfied with a change in the status of students or professors or the reform of the administration, whether planned or already put into operation. Those involved are convinced that the university cannot be saved by reforms in those three sectors, and the real question is the nature of the university as an institution.[5] The university has already been declared dead,[6] and people are quite sure that it will never rise again in its old form.[7]

If it were merely a matter of reforming, it would be enough to adapt the institution, which in its present form dates from the period of German idealism (von Humboldt), to the requirements of our present age, and to correct or replace such institutional defects as exist. Revolution is felt as the only solution when an analysis of the situation shows that it is beyond adaptation by simple development, and when the terms of reference which justified the existing institution are no longer valid, so that it should be swept away as soon as possible, by violence if necessary, to be replaced by something new. This again creates a moral problem. When should an institution be violently overthrown and the social order endangered in order to replace it by something new? The formal answer of the magisterium usually is that it is permissible only in case of an ultimate threat to the general well-being of the State or a group of the population. Is this general well-being threatened by the established institution of the university as it exists today? And if so, is this danger warded off by the university revolution as we in fact observe it today? The moral question then becomes: Is this revolution a move in the right direction or an outlet? If it is only an outlet, then revolution becomes in fact the best regulator in the hands of the establishment. But

[5] P. Ricoeur, "Réforme et révolution dans l'université," in *Esprit* 36 (June-July 1968), pp. 987-1002.
[6] P. Nonet, "La mort de l'université," in *La Revue Nouvelle* 25 (1969), pp. 5-14.
[7] E. Egger, "Gymnase et université en révolution," in *Choisir* 105-6 (1968), pp. 7-11; Barzun, *op. cit.*, is more hopeful in spite of his frank analysis of the American university: "For my part, I keep an unruffled faith in it, coupled with a conviction of the miserable deficiencies that exist."

the university revolution is not merely concerned with the university itself but with society, the established order which made this university possible and handles it as a power structure. If, therefore, the university revolution wants to be an effective movement, it must express social criticism effectively and, in practice, turn against the established order with a reasonable alternative to replace it.[8]

An outsider may find it strange that so much public attention is turned to the university revolution. Is the importance not exaggerated because an elite group is involved? The answer is "no", since there is an obvious analogy between the workers' revolution of socialism and Marxism [9] and the university revolution. In our society science has become the most prominent means of production, as the brute labor force was in the Marxist revolution. As Marxism accused capitalism of exploiting the laborer and thus alienating him, so the university revolution accuses the State and industry, whether Marxist or capitalist in orientation, of exploiting the scientist and technologist and alienating them, for both State and industry manipulate science in view of production and power. When science has thus become purely functional, it becomes alienated from itself.

Thus it is an inner necessity which makes the university revolution turn against the State and against industry.[10] For the rev-

---

[8] Insofar as the moving force of the French university revolution is concerned, Cohn Bendit rejects all leadership in the book he wrote with his brother Gabriel, *Obsolete Communism. The Left-Wing Alternative* (New York, 1968), p. 131; his intention is to keep a revolutionary situation alive, "unencumbered by the usual chains of command"; he blames the dogmatic character of the Communist Party for the failure of the May revolution.

[9] If, according to Pius XI, "the alienation of the workers from the Church is one of the greatest scandals of the 20th century", the Church will have to draw a conclusion from the Marxist revolution to the university revolution if she wants to avoid a total alienation of the intelligentsia from the Church.

[10] For an extensive report on this, see our article, "Prophets in the Secular City," in *Concilium* 37 (1968), pp. 133-50; cf. L. Armand and M. Drancourt, *Le pari européen* (Paris, 1968), pp. 20-79 and 146-49; R. Bernard, "Une libération," in *Economie et Humanisme* 183 (Oct. 1968), pp. 68-70.

olution the main issue is: Who will manipulate mankind's intellectual potential and the sciences in the future? [11] The university revolution pleads for a new autonomy of science.[12] The university as an institution may still give the impression of being independent because of its privileges and the right to live by its own usages, but in actual fact it is tied to various vested interests.[13] Just as Marxism wanted to see the laborers in control of their own potential,[14] so the leaders of the student protest movements want to see the scientists and students in control of the intellectual potential by means of their own councils and unions, and thus create an as yet unknown autonomy for science. Here, once again, we touch on an ethical problem: the question of who should control science which is by nature free. So far, the facts as we have been given them have not yet provided an answer. But it is already clear that there can be no question of an absolute autonomy, since both research and the whole business of a university are not by themselves productive to such an extent that they can be economically self-sufficient, and such an economic dependence will probably always remain inevitable.

What has been said should already have made it clear that the roots of the university revolution lie deeper. The fact that the social unrest among students, professors and members of the administrative body has at a given moment exploded in Berkeley or Naterre is merely accidental in this perspective. Moreover,

[11] M. A. Luyten and others, *Recherche et culture. Tâches d'une université catholique* (Fribourg, 1965), pp. 121-35, where H. Schmidinger gives a brief survey of recent literature about the origin of the medieval university; H. R. Sonntag, "Versuch über die Latein-Amerikanischen Universitäten," in *Kursbuch* 13 (1968), pp. 108-26.

[12] "University Autonomy," in *I.A.U. Papers* 7 (1965), p. 1: "It is evident that, in the context of modern society, no university makes or can make a claim to complete autonomy. It derives its legal existence from an act of some external authority, usually the State, and its instrument of incorporation prescribes in some detail what it may do and what it may not do—for example, in relation to its property or its dealing with other institutions or even with its own members."

[13] F. Bowels, *Access to Higher Education* (New York, 1963).

[14] U.D.U.A.L., *Latin-American University Legislation* (Mexico, 1967), p. 47; for the autonomy of Russian universities, see the article by G. W. Vodchenko in *I.A.U.*, *op. cit.*, pp. 121-22.

already in 1917 an attempt was made in Cordoba (Argentine) to set up new structures in the university, in a way which looks very much like what most participants in the revolution today have vaguely in mind for the future: [15] a university which rests democratically on the people as a whole. Ideologically speaking, the university revolution is the last consequence drawn from the French Revolution and has issued from the Marxist laborers' revolution. Because the university as an institution clearly betrays its Western origins, the decolonization factor must be added to the other already mentioned factors of the university revolution in some regions. This considerably changes the character of the revolution in some countries in South America, Africa, India and the Middle East. We propose, therefore, to begin with some documentation about the international character of this revolution, and then to pass on to the effect of this on present thinking about the statute and function of the Catholic university; finally, we will ask ourselves what future image of the university emerges from all this in recent publications, and what contribution the Catholic university can make in this field.

I

How International Is the University
Revolution in Actual Fact?

An international publication like *Concilium* is always faced with the difficulty of finding out how international the facts are which provide the material for its documentation. At first sight this does not seem difficult where the university revolution is concerned. There is no longer any university where the revolution is not tugging at the established structures in one way or another. In appearance it looks the same everywhere. A closer look, however, reveals significant differences, because the place of the university in society and its connections with vested interest groups differ widely from one nation to another. We can, in spite of this,

[15] H. R. Sonntag, *art. cit.*, in *Kursbuch*, p. 110.

distinguish four regions which each show their own peculiar features in the overall pattern of the revolution. They are: (1) North America and Western Europe; (2) Latin America; (3) the developing countries; (4) the Marxist countries. In this last case we must sharply distinguish between the cultural revolution within Chinese Marxism and the student protest movement within dogmatic Marxism, as, for instance, in Poland.

1. *North America and Western Europe*

When, as is usual, the function of a university is seen as three-fold—namely, formation, teaching and research—the general dissatisfaction in this region is principally directed against the way in which research is handicapped. This may sound improbable because—certainly in the United States, at least—the greatest amount of money is spent in this field of research.[16] But the revolution here is directed against the way in which industry, the State and the university are bound up with each other, although even a revolutionary recognizes the fact that a close link between State, university and industry ensures economic and technological prosperity. The resentment here is with the fact that the choice of research (in itself boundless) is determined by the principle of utility: Does it serve productivity and technological and economic progress? This functional interpretation of research also affects the financial support given to research. It is obvious that the major industries which, together with the defense (or war) apparatus of the State, are the main financial providers will only support such research as is useful to those industries and defense. This is the reason why the problems of underdevelopment and the war in Vietnam are constantly mentioned in the revolutionary debate.[17]

[16] McGregor, "The Future of the Catholic University," a paper read at the eighth assembly of the FIUC (Kinshasa, 1968), fol. 3. We have used several of these papers, put at our disposal by the delegate for Nijmegen University, Prof. H. J. Lammers.
[17] "Origine et sens du mouvement," in *Esprit* (June-July 1968), pp. 1046-79.

2. Latin America

In Latin America the university revolution concentrates mainly on attacking the university as the institution of a privileged elite.[18] The possibility for anyone with the required ability to study there may well exist in most Latin American States, but the necessary pre-conditions simply are not there. Elementary education is weak, and secondary education is in practice not available for intelligent children from the working class. These shortcomings are, in their turn, due to the permanent refusal of the established authorities to undertake a genuine industrialization of their countries. One can see why Latin American capitalists are not particularly keen on investing a great deal of money in setting up their industries in their own countries. They prefer to leave this to the United States and are content with providing the raw materials. This means that the proletariat remains stagnant, since the technicians for the existing industries are trained in the United States. No attempt is made to start a movement in their own universities at home which would develop the faculties in a way that could produce results in this field comparable to those achieved in Western Europe, the United States and especially in Russia. What North Americans like to call a contribution to the economic development in these countries is called economic imperialism by the students of South America. Therefore, the university revolution consists mainly in creating the possibility for the proletariat to develop in one way or another. This may create the impression outside of communist infiltration, but in reality it is an attempt made to develop the intellectual potential of the people.

This protest against an elite university shows still another fea-

[18] I. Rosier, "Het non-conformisme van de Latijns-Amerikaanse universiteiten als stem van het volk in zijn drang naar ontwikkeling," and "Latijns Amerika geconfronteerd met Europa en Noord-Amerika door invloed van eenzelfde technificering" (1968); A. Birou, "Signification politique d'une révolte," in Economie et Humanisme 182 (July-Aug. 1968), pp. 74-79.

ture. There are State universities, and these are better equipped than many so-called small universities. However, the small universities are only accessible to the intelligentsia from the upper layers of the oligarchy. The State universities' catching area covers only ten percent of the intellectual potential. The small oligarchical universities, where no revolutionary sound is ever heard, take in the intelligentsia of the upper class, and the rest are simply excluded from any university training. The small universities feed the governmental framework (law, economics, sociology), whereas students of State universities are threatened by unemployment at the end of their studies. This situation does not result from a saturated labor market for intellectuals as such. On the contrary, there is a lack of medical doctors, technologists and academically trained forces, because no student after graduation can expect a career in the non-industrialized countryside which has no economy, no prosperity and little cultural life; thus even the most idealistic intellectual is likely to suffer a mental breakdown. Intellectuals who at the end of their studies cannot find suitable employment in a town will spread rebelliousness among students exposed to the same fate. The most outspoken and rebellious students come from the upper middle classes and, they are willingly listened to by their colleagues from the lower classes.[19]

Rosier has experienced the university situation of Latin America, and as a European he can compare it with the situation in Western Europe; he found that, in spite of much idealism, even among students from the oligarchic milieu, the university revolution of Latin America shows negative, rancorous and even pathological features. There are indeed pressure groups, but the positive projects of the country's progress do not come from them. They are and remain in the hands of the dominant classes. According to him there is a lack of leadership and of a clear ideal for the future, and there is too much concern with breaking with the past. To satisfy the spiritual and cultural hunger of a great people, Latin America needs restructuring. To give a

[19] Rosier, art. cit., fol. 14.

people a cultural and academic training, without creating the material conditions required to make this training effective, actually aggravates the already existing frustration and the intensification of the spirit of non-conformity and revolution which is rampant.

3. *The Developing Countries*

In the developing countries the institutional university is seen as the product of Western power; it turns out an intelligentsia unfit for the home country, and so lures them away to countries where they are not required but where they can find better employment. The university was born and grew up in Europe, and during the last century it has greatly developed in the United States. It has shown great historical maturity, has vast cultural wealth and has developed great powers in the control of nature—things that are envied by the intelligentsia of developing countries, but in practice incapable of full realization outside Europe, because elsewhere the vast majority of the people still think in rather primitive terms. The universities in those countries provide the intelligentsia with a takeoff point to European or American universities. This hampers the expansion of the universities in developing countries, often set up by ecclesiastical or industrial enterprise.

Yet, even in these still young and not fully adult universities, not yet adjusted to an international level, there is a revolution of sorts. Some have tried to dispose of this with the assertion that it is all mere imitation of universities in Western Europe and the United States,[20] a status symbol and a declaration of solidarity with a worldwide movement,[21] but it is more likely that we are seeing here a protest against the creaming-off process which lures intellectuals away from these regions. This process has often been depicted as a political manipulation by the great industrial powers who are convinced that Western Europe and America

---

[20] O. Massing, "Achtzehn Thesen zum Verhältniss von Universität und Gesellschaft," in *Hochland* 60 (1967-68), pp. 662-67.

[21] L. Armand and M. Brancourt, *op. cit.*, p. 163.

must produce the ideas for which the developing countries are to be allowed to provide the labor force.[22] The hypothesis that these revolutions are exploited by Marxism to bring about a world revolution is disproved by the fact that in the university circles of these developing countries Marxism is clearly unable to persuade the intelligentsia to stay.[23] The most obvious reasons for the revolution here seem to lie in the low level of the lecturing staff and the corruption in the administration of these universities. If teaching, training and research are the three functions of a modern university, these universities still lack so much in the first function of teaching that this provides more than sufficient motive to create unrest among students, and this unrest will mold itself on the European or American model.

4. *The Marxist Countries*

If at first the Russian revolution left the universities alone, from the 1930's the university became an instrument in the hands of the State. Nobody doubts the high intellectual level of these universities, but we are ill-informed about the resistance to the resulting functionalization of the Russian universities. We know a little more about two explosions of student unrest, one in Czechoslovakia and one in Poland,[24] and in Russia itself students spread pamphlets against various Soviet governments. In the Soviet Union the Western university revolution is seen on the one hand as a continuation of the Russian revolution, but on the other it is exposed as a New Left ideology, a utopian, anarchic and anti-communist tendency.[25] The university revolution in the Soviet Union itself and in the countries of the Warsaw Pact mainly shows a demand for political freedom and an awareness of national cultures. In Russia itself it also turns against a curious application of the "limited number" system. In this

---

[22] *Quelle université? Quelle société?* (Paris, 1968), p. 64.

[23] Cf. Abalah Dagher, paper for FIUC (*loc. cit.*, 1968).

[24] "Studenten in Prag," in *Kursbuch* 13 (1968), p. 67; "Warschauer Bilanz," p. 91; on p. 106 it is said that "the documents show an extremely limited view, and their political substance is thin".

[25] N. Moltschanov, *op. cit.* (see footnote 2).

system the secondary school diploma allows a Russian student to sit for a competitive examination for higher education. A previously fixed number of the best students are then admitted. The others can, if they wish, pursue a higher education by means of correspondence courses or evening classes. This system certainly makes it possible to select the future specialists while leaving the door open for others.

Because of a materialistic ideology, the sciences are emphasized in the Marxist countries. As in the United States and in Western Europe, the faculties of philosophy, sociology, history and economics appear to be the centers of opposition against the unscientific handling of these disciplines of the mind. The pronounced linking of university teaching with the organization of labor also seems to provoke some protest among the students, but this is soon suppressed. This suppression is easier because of the lack of student interest in politics, due to the influence of the present regime.[26]

China's "cultural revolution", carried out by the young Chinese intelligentsia, shows a different character. Originally Mao seems to have meant them to be the brain trust of the Chinese revolution and the representatives of China's own type of Marxism. From 1967 on, however, the regime has switched its hopes again to the laborers and soldiers.[27] It seems rather improbable that the new China will grant a genuine freedom of speech in the foreseeable future. The repression is harsh; students are being condemned to military service and forced labor with the peasants without any hope of being allowed again to enter the university.[28]

What part does the Catholic university play in the revolution

[26] For bibliography, see DIC Bulletin 1, 4 (Dec. 1968), p. 124: "Universiteit [student] en politiek".

[27] G. Melis, art. cit., pp. 346-60. Since 1955 a total of 40 million students have been sent to the countryside, some temporarily, some for good. There is a campaign to encourage the rural training of students. According to the American National Science Foundation, China has at present 15 million students or young people who can be counted as such.

[28] L. Trivière, "Les chrétiens devant le défi chinois," in Inf. Cath. Int. 329 (Feb. 1, 1969), p. 31.

in these four regions? In many countries there is none at all. In connection with the cultural revolution in China, it has been pointed out that there has been no Catholic influence on Chinese development because of the lack of a Catholic university. The Fu Yen university of Formosa, with 2,493 students, can no longer exercise any influence and is identified with "Western capitalism".

With regard to the remaining regions, there is first of all the strikingly uneven distribution of Catholic universities in the regions. In the first there are 93, in the second 45, in the developing countries 6, and in the Marxist countries there is only the Catholic university of Lublin with 1,698 students. Perhaps one should also mention the Catholic university of Dalàt (500 students) in South Vietnam, but this is only ten years old.

Of most Catholic universities one may say that they still aim at what Pope Paul VI said in his letter of congratulations to the university of Dalàt: ". . . the training of competent teachers and teams as well as an aid to the deepening of the faith of young Christians and the active manifestation of their charity." [29] But the university revolution is precisely opposed to such institutional training as the purpose of a university. Most States see their universities as training schools for their administrative and economic establishment and higher education as training for the management of industry. It is therefore not astonishing that the Churches, too, saw the university in that light. This phase, however, seems to have passed and is in any case severely criticized by the protest movement. The movements in Nijmegen and Washington can be seen in this perspective, and the same holds for the student movement at the Gregorian University in Rome. For the rest, Rome seems to steer toward one or two genuinely scientific universities instead of a multiplicity of small theological faculties.[30] In South America most Catholic universities belong

[29] *L'Osservatore Romano* 109 (Feb. 7, 1969), p. 1.

[30] "Quelques normes en vue de la révision de la Constitution apostolique 'Deus scientiarum Dominus' sur les études académiques ecclésiastiques," in *La Doc. Cath.* 51 (Jan. 1969), pp. 64-75; "Le cardinal Garrone présente des lignes directrices pour la réforme," in *Inf. Cath. Int.* 316 (1968), pp. 15-16.

to the category of small universities where there is no trouble. Catholics at the State universities, mainly drawn from the lower middle class and the working class, take an active part in the student revolution. Interesting is the changing attitude of Catholics in East Germany; [31] from being uninterested in university affairs, they have become more active now that even the severely Marxist structures of the East German State universities have proved to be also exposed to the effects of the revolutionary movements. In France, where the revolution reached a high standard, Catholic students not only took an active part in the demonstrations but also in the theory and motives behind the May revolution.[32] After some hesitation the Catholic hierarchy also adopted a positive attitude toward the protest, so that in some parochial communities the movement began to live and became a topic for sermons. The Dutch experiment of the "student Church" seems to have issued from the protest movement because the general dissatisfaction with the close connection of the university to the establishment spread to the ecclesiastical establishment.

In the United States and Canada the Catholic universities unconsciously contributed to one of the aims of the student revolution, the democratization of higher education. When Catholicism came to America, the Protestant Churches already had their universities. The Catholics, who usually were the underdogs of American society, acquired national prestige by taking both higher and lower education into their own hands. This gave a

---

[31] "Studentenschaft und Hochschulgemeinden der DDR," in *Herder Korrespondenz* 22 (1968), pp. 312-15: "At the moment we have the extraordinary fact that the majority of Catholic students are found in the scientific and medical faculties. The fact of a relatively lesser representation there of Catholic students in the West German Federation prompts the question whether Catholics are not disposed to study these subjects or have been given a wrong attitude by the Church toward them, and the answer is given here, at least partly." Moreover, it shows "what an unrealistic view the Church leaders have of a Christian's need for information".

[32] J. Mansir, "Les chrétiens français devant une situation révolutionnaire (mai-juin 1968)," in *IDO-C* 68-48 (Nov. 17, 1968), fol. 3; "Les chrétiens dans la révolution," in *Inf. Cath. Int.* 314 (June 1968), pp. 5-20; "Chrétiens en mai '68," in *Christus* 60 (Oct. 1968), pp. 438-53.

fair section of the population access to the universities, something which, for instance, never happened in Latin America.

In general one may say that the Catholic universities as such were more conservative than progressive. Officially the university was seen as a means for the apostolate and as a counterweight to the State universities. Like all "free" universities they are at present in an unfavorable economic situation compared with the State universities. Their students, however, have played no less a part in the protest movement than students from other universities.[33]

II

THE STATUTE AND FUNCTION OF THE CATHOLIC UNIVERSITY

Up until recently the statute of the Catholic university was quite clear. It was a university, bound as an institution to the Catholic Church. A careful study of the reports of the Congress about the future of the Catholic university, organized by the *Fédération Internationale des Universités Catholiques* (F.I.U.C.) in the Congo in 1968,[34] shows that there are widely divergent views about a Catholic university—for example, a university founded and controlled by the Catholic hierarchy; an independent university as distinct from a State university; a university which lets itself be guided by the magisterium; a university which protects the faith of professors and students; an elite university; a university which is meant to be the crown of Catholic culture. These views have lost practically all their obvious significance,

[33] P. Henle. "The American Catholic University," FIUC paper for the Congo assembly of 1968, fol. 16 and 18. On fol. 30 he says that non-Catholic lecturers maintain that they are left more freedom in Catholic universities than elsewhere, and in fol. 39 he discusses the idea that the Catholic university is in transition.

[34] Compare the opinions of Rooney, Torralba, L. Scherz Alba, H. Carrier, C. Mendez de Almeida (the Catholic university must be integrated in a new policy for education) and Luyten in their respective papers for the FIUC assembly of 1968.

even in Latin America.[35] There remains nevertheless a relatively general conviction that the achievement of the Catholic university should not simply vanish. There is an awareness which stresses the character of the university as such rather than its Catholicity,[36] without even dreaming of a wholly independent university.

Generally speaking, we can distinguish two tendencies. One, well illustrated by Luyten's article in this volume, looks for this Catholicity of a university in a Catholic-inspired view of the world. In that case, a genuine unity of inspiration would pervade the various disciplines and express the ideal conception of the unity of all sciences as seen in the light of the faith. Here the faith is seen as a particular source of knowledge; over against the totality of knowledge the Catholic has the advantage of a special source of knowledge which complements the other one. This is still close to von Humboldt's view which dominated the German State universities for more than a century: a unity of professors, a unity of students, a unity of all sciences which, supported by the disinterested assistance of the State, will have the monopoly of science. Since the Americanization of the university, which also affected the European universities, this view has been overtaken by the democratization and political integration of the university. Another view sees this Catholicity in what is a precondition for all science: the spontaneous awareness of oneself in the world, the only approach to any science.[37] When the student

[35] P. Furter, "Amérique Latine: jeunesse et politique," in *Choisir* 9 (Sept. 1968), pp. 10-17. In his "Die Verantwortung des Studenten für die Kultur," in *Die Verantwortung der Universität* (Würzburg, 1954), pp. 5-35, R. Guardini had already pointed out the danger of protectionism.

[36] M. de Certeau, "Mai 1968," in *Etudes* (Oct. 1968), pp. 463-70; *idem*, "Savoir et société," in *Esprit* 36 (Oct. 1968), pp. 292-312; J. Ladriere, "L'université et l'Eglise de Wallonie," in *La Revue Nouvelle* 24 (Dec. 1968), pp. 528-34.

[37] Unfortunately the definitive report of the Schillebeeckx commission on the Catholic university of Nijmegen has not yet appeared. See, however, his article in *Recherche et culture* (Fribourg, 1965), pp. 33-45, and F. Theunis, "Katholieke universiteit?" in *Kultuurleven* 33 (Nov. 1966), pp. 691-704. A description can be found in the FIUC papers referred to: ". . . a community of persons differing in experience and function, equal

revolution speaks about professional idiots and about students as "trained subjects" (*Untertanenfabrik*), the university will have to think again about the human aspects of science. Every science derives its human aspects from the original human experience in which it is rooted. If the university wants to remain human, it will have to reintegrate the sciences in the original integral experience where faith, too, belongs. A science without values (*wertfrei*) is impossible. The original experience influences the whole attempt of a university to attain to truth and science. The original pre-reflexive experience affects not only each positive science, but also the interdisciplinary approach and the philosophical attitude. The university thus points again to a specific view of the world—in this case, the Christian view. The conscious experience of "being in the world" is therefore the foundation and the root of both science and faith. By its nature, faith requires science and the university because otherwise it can no longer assert itself as an authentic and contemporary faith. When the believing community examines this question with a sense of moral responsibility, it will not only lead to theology but also to a universal science (*universitas scientiarum*).

It should already be clear that such an approach does not intend to encourage the faithful to contribute more to still more Catholic universities. It reflects the factual trend not to extend the number of Catholic universities and to think before actually setting up another one. The tendency is rather to coordinate the existing smaller Catholic universities. This second tendency has an explicit connection with various elements that are prominent in the general protest movement in the universities and which are described as political Christianity. It presupposes the presence of Catholic universities and refuses to become anonymous, but it looks for new perspectives. It rather thinks in terms of a specific

---

in dignity, devoted to scientific research and the integral formation of man, and finding their inspiration for whatever task they fulfill in the light of revealed truth, and so a community that creates a center for the development and diffusion of an authentic Christian culture."

form of the "critical" university which fits in with the social criticism of society as a function of Christianity today. To have or to build a Catholic university is then seen not so much as a privilege to be insisted upon or an unalienable right, but rather as a task to which Christianity is committed. From being a matter of juridical privilege the Catholic university has shifted to a question of ethical imperative.[38]

III

How Catholic Should the Future University Be?

When one wades through the stream of publications issuing from the conflict in the universities (it has already been called the "paper revolution"), one constantly meets the assertion that there is as yet no university.[39] The questions concerning the structure of this university of the future have received various answers. L. Jerphagon has recently tried to outline a sketch of tomorrow's university: the whole teaching program to be composed and introduced by the students; the courses to be given by professors chosen by the students on the basis of various political criteria; no periodical checks or examinations; academic degrees to be automatic for as long as society wants them; the courses to be subdivided into projects of actual interest (not the mere passing on of a parcel of past human knowledge); the projects to be worked out in groups; anybody can join the university without entrance examinations; a suitable salary to be paid to the students for the duration of their studies. If one looks for something more detailed and concrete, one discovers two tendencies in this search for tomorrow's university.

[38] J. Julliard, "Syndicalisme révolutionnaire et révolution étudiante," in *Esprit* (June-July 1968), pp. 1037-45.

[39] J. J. Natanson, "La réforme d'Edgar Faure," in *Esprit* (Nov. 1968), p. 544: "There are only professional high schools (the faculties) and the university as the whole *ensemble* of education."

1. If we follow Marcuse,[40] the answer to the theory that the realization of one-dimensional man in a welfare society must imply a new system of communicating human knowledge lies in the impersonal computers which will enable the man of the future to satisfy the demands of a continuous learning process. In a penetrating study, Chirpaz [41] has pointed out that the perfectioning of one-dimensional man must lead to a one-dimensional society, which would mean the death of man himself; thus after the death of God we would run into the death of man. To satisfy man's desire in this sense by means of a perfectly industrialized society would alienate man from the real dimension of his desire and hence from his initiative, his creativity and his task which is to continue the humanization of the world. This failure to appreciate the spanning force of man's desire would lead to a narcissistic society, so that in his one-dimensional universe he would only meet himself and never the "really other".

There would be no genuine ethic. For Marcuse there is only the economic social problem, and there is no such thing as the general social problem of man's independence within the lasting dependence on others.[42] He does not understand that man basically needs his fellow man, not only for the provision of economic means, but also for finding a meaning to his own life, and even for the development of his self-awareness. And so he never comes to grips with the problem of people's life together, a problem which constantly demands new solutions and which is precisely the problem confronting the university. The university rev-

[40] The secret of Marcuse's appeal seems to lie in an attractive mixture of Freud, Marx and American sociology: G. Decke, "Die theoretische Basis von Marcuses Geschichtsphilosophie und Gesellschaftstheorie. Freuds psychoanalytische Anthropologie als Marxismus-Ersatz?" in *Zeitschr. f. Evang. Ethik* 12 (Nov. 1968), pp. 372-77; W. Schweitzer, "Die Theologie der Revolution. H. Marcuse und die Studenten," in *Evang. Ethik* (May 1968), pp. 174-81; R. McNamara, "Students and Power," in *Thought* 42 (1968), pp. 202-10; W. D. Marsch, "Utopie der Befreiung und christliche Freiheit. Theologischer Versuch über H. Marcuse," *loc. cit.*, pp. 17-34.

[41] F. Chirpaz, "Aliénation et utopie," in *Esprit* 36 (Jan. 1969), pp. 74-88.

[42] H. Hoefnagels, "Marcuse," in *Streven* 22 (Nov. 1968), p. 135.

olution then degenerates into a mere game. But the human effort, whether in labor or in study, cannot be reduced to a game by social progress: it remains an ethical issue which makes heavy demands on man if he wants to attain to genuine freedom and not slide into slavery.

2. Cohn Bendit seems to seek the solution in ignoring the question of the structure of the new university.[43] According to him the sole mission of the university revolution lies in perpetuating the situation of conflict and revolution as the only fertile soil out of which the university of tomorrow will rise naturally. This is an evasion and a refusal to face the intellectual effort required to discover the possibility of this future university. This problem is not solved by abolishing the distinction between professors and students and calling them seniors and juniors cooperating in a team. This exposes us to inefficiency in the mangement of university affairs. The spontaneous generation of the university of the future is utopian.

In both cases one gets the impression that man, having succeeded in changing a despotic nature from a threat into a force that serves him, will now see in this technological world a kind of new "nature" with the same magic tyranny over him as the previous uncontrolled primitive nature. The moral task of humanizing this second nature will remain, even though at first it looks just as impossible as it did to primitive man ever to be able to control the threat of a nature on which he depended. He would land himself again in a fatal, though scientifically understood, necessity which would again impose its anonymous and even despotic scientifically-known laws on man, and so alienate him once again from himself. He might no longer be a primitive slave or a proletarian in such a situation, but he would still be manipulated by a new force, beyond and above himself. This force would then no longer be called capitalism but impersonal knowl-

---

[43] *La fin de l'utopie* (Paris, 1968), p. 15: "Radical transformation is that which introduces the aesthetic-erotic dimension"; A. Clair, "Une philosophie de la nature," in *Esprit* 36 (Jan. 1969), p. 55: "La totale positivité d'éros selon Marcuse."

edge. This would become—and in Marcuse's case already is—so oppressive that the possibility of deliverance from scientific structures would no longer be thinkable, with the result that his one-dimensional humanity condemns man to an inevitable fate.

3. Could it be the task of a Catholic university—or, rather, of Christianity—to break through this scientific fatalism with scientific means and through a constantly renewed belief in redemption? Several Cathloic scholars have pointed in this direction. Christian hope could become an inspiration for research, the weakest spot in the university world of today, as is clear from practically all the forms of the conflict. Christianity's contribution to the university of tomorrow might be the scientific practice of multi-dimensional man. The essence of man does not lie only in what is, but above all in what is not yet, what still lies in the future, and what man is still lacking. Tomorrow's university would then be neither Catholic, nor State, nor Marxist, but, in Professor Metz's sense,[44] political, which is more than merely critical. In exercising this critical function, including at the scientific level, Christianity's contribution could be irreplaceable. Just as, in this context the French Revolution was symbolized by the seizure of the Bastille (symbol of power), so the university revolution could be symbolized by the seizure of the word (symbol of man's rational nature), as long as this word becomes "man" in the future.

[44] R. van der Gucht, "Le visage futur de l'université catholique," in *La Revue Nouvelle* 47 (Jan. 1968), pp. 30-32; L. Ladrière, "Pour une conception organique de l'université catholique," in *Nouv. Rev. Théol.* 100 (Feb. 1966), pp. 155-72.

BIOGRAPHICAL NOTES

JEAN-MARIE AUBERT: Born in France in 1916, he was ordained in 1946. He studied in France at the Major Seminary of Fréjus and at the University of Strasbourg, and in Rome at the Gregorian. He holds degrees in theology and Canon Law, and is professor of moral theology at the faculty of Catholic theology in the University of Strasbourg. He is also an honorary canon of Toulon. His publications include *Recherche scientifique et foi chrétienne* (Paris, 1962) and *Loi de Dieu, lois des hommes* (Paris, 1964).

NORBERT LUYTEN, O.P.: Born in Belgium in 1909, he was ordained in 1933. He studied at various scholasticates of his Order and at the Major Institute of Philosophy of Louvain. He received his doctorate in philosophy in 1943, and since 1945 he has been professor of philosophy at the University of Fribourg in Switzerland. His published works include *Teilhard de Chardin, Nouvelles perspectives du savoir* (Fribourg, 1965) and *Recherche et Culture* (Paris, 1965).

HENK LINNEBANK: Born in Amsterdam in 1926, he is a Catholic. Holding a degree in social and political science, he is joint-secretary of the Christian International Union of Business Executives, and delegate-general of the European Committee of Cooperation with Latin America.

HERMANN WALLRAFF, S.J.: Born in Germany in 1913, he was ordained in 1944. He studied at the universities of Munich, Bonn and Cologne, receiving his doctorate in political science. He is professor of social ethics at the Major College of philosophy and theology of Sankt Georgen in Germany. His published works include *Eigentumspolitik, Arbeit und Mitbestimmung* (Cologne, 1968).

FRANCISCUS TELLEGEN: Born in Holland in 1904, he is a Catholic. He studied in Holland at the Major Technical College of Delft, and is a chemical engineer who holds a doctorate in technical science. Since 1965 he has been professor of philosophy at the Major Technical College of Eindhoven. He is the author of numerous articles on Christianity in the modern world.

RUDOLF KAUTZKY: Born in Vienna in 1913, he is a Catholic. A doctor of medicine, he has been director of the department of neuro-surgery at the University Clinic of Neurology at Hamburg-Eppendorf in Germany since 1967. His publications include "Die ärztliche Manipulation des menschlichen Lebens" in *Umschau in Wissenschaft und Technik* (1968).

WILLEM ARIËNS: Born in Amsterdam in 1899, he is a Catholic. He studied at the University of Utrecht, and has a degree in law. Since 1956 he has been president of the Court of Appeals at Bois-le-Duc in the Netherlands.

JOSÉ-MARÍA SOLOZÁBAL: Born in Spain in 1921, he was ordained in 1953. He studied at the seminary in Vitoria and at the University of Madrid. He received his doctorate in political and economic science in 1957, and is currently professor of political economy at the University of Deusto, Bilbao.

WILHELM KORFF: Born in Germany in 1926, he was ordained in 1952. He studied at the Major Seminary of Cologne and at the University of Bonn, receiving his doctorate in theology in 1965. He holds a scholarship in the German Scientific Research Service. His thesis *Ehre, Prestige, Gewissen* was published in Cologne in 1966.

THEO BEEMER: Born in the Netherlands in 1927, he was ordained in 1952. He studied at the universities of Nijmegen, Louvain and Munich, receiving his doctorate in theology. Since 1966 he has been a lecturer in moral theology at the University of Nijmegen. His publications include *De kerk van morgen* (Roermond, 1966).

International Publishers of CONCILIUM

ENGLISH EDITION
Paulist Press
Paramus, N.J., U.S.A.

Burns & Oates Ltd.
25 Ashley Place
London, S.W.1

DUTCH EDITION
Uitgeverij Paul Brand, N.V.
Hilversum, Netherlands

FRENCH EDITION
Maison Mame
Tours/Paris, France

JAPANESE EDITION (PARTIAL)
Nansôsha
Tokyo, Japan

GERMAN EDITION
Verlagsanstalt Benziger & Co., A.G.
Einsiedeln, Switzerland

Matthias Grunewald-Verlag
Mainz, W. Germany

SPANISH EDITION
Ediciones Guadarrama
Madrid, Spain

PORTUGUESE EDITION
Livraria Morais Editora, Ltda.
Lisbon, Portugal

ITALIAN EDITION
Editrice Queriniana
Brescia, Italy

POLISH EDITION (PARTIAL)
Pallottinum
Poznan-Warsaw, Poland

DATE DUE